HORNCHURCH, ELM PARK & HAROLD WOOD

THROUGH TIME

Brian Evans

AMBERLEY PUBLISHING

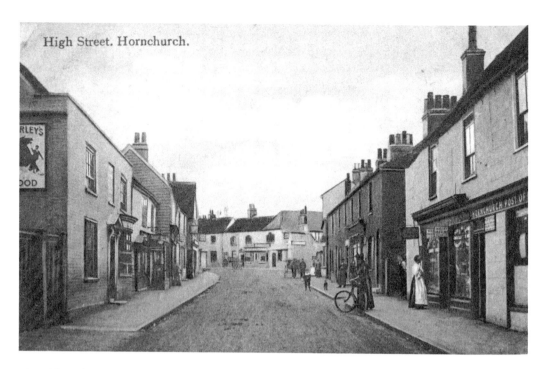

High Street. Hornchurch.

The old High Street, Hornchurch in 1904. A coloured postcard probably taken from an original photograph by Frank Luff of the top end of the White Hart portion of the street, northwest of the hostelry. On the left are buildings removed in 1956 to widen this part of the street. This card was published by J.W. Wilfred, Tobacconist. On the right is the Post Office and straight ahead the Britannia building on the corner of North Street.

First published 2010

Amberley Publishing Plc
Cirencester Road, Chalford,
Stroud, Gloucestershire, GL6 8PE

www.amberley-books.com

Copyright © Brian Evans, 2010

The right of Brian Evans to be identified as the
Author of this work has been asserted in accordance
with the Copyrights, Designs and Patents Act 1988.

ISBN 978 1 84868 633 5

British Library Cataloguing in Publication Data.
A catalogue record for this book is available from
the British Library.

Typeset in 9.5pt on 12pt Celeste.
Typesetting by Amberley Publishing.
Printed in the UK.

Every effort has been made to trace copyright holders. The author apologises for any errors or omissions
and would be grateful to be notified of any corrections that should be incorporated in future reprints or
editions of this book

Introduction

HORNCHURCH. The official guide of 1962 describes the area's past – "it would be difficult to find within 20 miles of London any place with more historical associations than Hornchurch. The parish formed a part of the ancient Royal Manor of Havering and at one time the whole of the Liberty of Havering was one civil and ecclesiastical parish with the name of Hornchurch."

But its history goes back even further. Hornchurch in fact lay at the very edge of the ice sheet which covered England in the last Great Ice Age. From that time successive inhabitants peopled the area more or less continuously. This perhaps included an early tribe led by a charismatic leader, Horn. After the arrival of the Normans, the medieval King Henry II sponsored in 1159 a priory on the hill where St Andrew's Church stands today. The name appears on documents as the 'Horned Monastery'. The priory was dissolved in 1391 and its possessions in Hornchurch were bought by William of Wykeham, Bishop of Winchester as part of an endowment for his foundation of New College Oxford. Over 500 documents at this college today record land deals made by the priory, giving an insight into medieval times locally. The village became famous for its leather goods and this led to the name 'Hornchurch' being reinforced by association with the cattle trade. Eventually the church acquired the unique distinction – that it was decorated at its east end by a pair of carved horns. Until the twentieth century the town had many ancient buildings from past centuries. A large number of those in the High Street and the remaining nucleus of the village were demolished, leaving us today with a few interesting survivors, e.g. those on the hill up to the church and some eighteenth century houses such as Langtons and Fairkytes.

HAROLD WOOD. An area at the extreme northern end of Hornchurch parish, named after the last Saxon king who owned the manor and other land around which once covered an extensive neighbourhood between Romford and Brentwood. Parts of this became subsumed into other areas later on. The new nucleus grew slowly from a hamlet to the present suburb. Early attempts to create new housing in the middle of the nineteenth century persuaded the Great Eastern Railway to provide a station at the bottom of Oak Road – originally only a halt where trains were flagged down if required. This is shown on the OS map of 1865. The King Harold Public House was built in 1868 to serve the original roads with Saxon-inspired names (Athelstan, Fitzilian, Ethelburga and

Alfred) leading off Gubbins Lane. It took until the twentieth century for the additions to appear and form a substantial suburb with a new station on the Gubbins Lane Bridge in the 1930s.

ELM PARK. A 1930s suburb created by the firm of Costain's on what had been farmland, at the centre of a triangle formed by Rainham Road, Hornchurch Road, and Abbs Cross Lane. Elm Farm had been mentioned in AD1610. The firm of Richard Costain purchased the cornfields and began to construct 20,000 reasonably built small houses, affordable to the working class. Some of the materials used were excavated on site. Some very attractive brochures were produced to lure potential buyers from their rented older housing nearer London. A nod was given to Garden Suburb principles. The great advantage of the site was the railway line running through and a new station was provided next to the planned shopping centre and close to the houses. The service was provided by an electrified District Line extension into Essex. The houses did not suit everybody but a successful suburb came into being from 1935, unaware that Hornchurch Airfield just to the south east was to play a pivotal role within four years due to the outbreak of World War II.

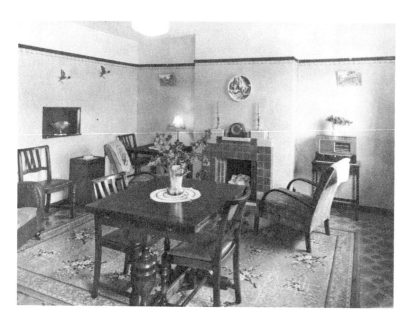

Some new housing after the war was designed by Hornchurch Urban District Council rather than Costain as Elm Park spread southwards from the railway. This is 83 Ambleside Avenue, Elm Park. Mrs Riley's living room was part of a postwar two bedroom maisonette. Note typical features of the time such as the serving hatch to kitchen on left and central carpet laid over linoleum floor covering. The furniture has the air of post-war utility plus of the 1940s/1950s period.

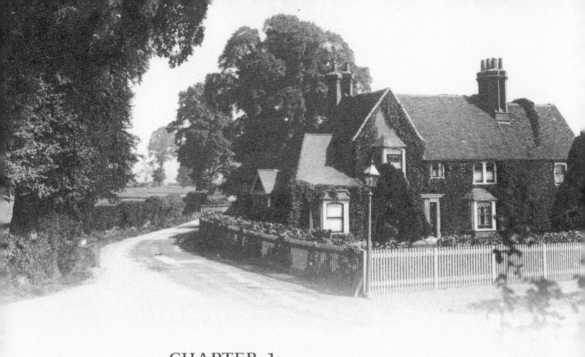

CHAPTER 1
The Village

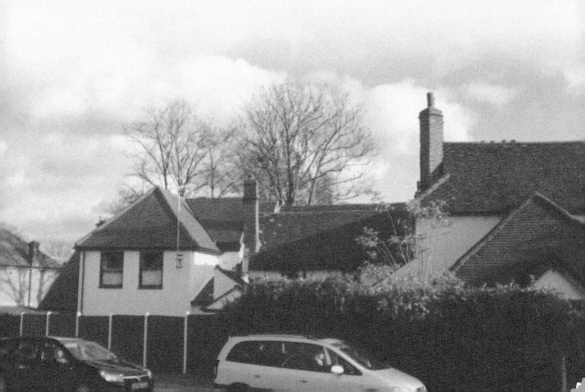

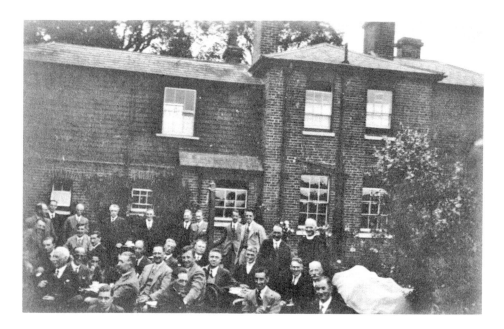

Chaplaincy Garden

The Chaplaincy garden with a men's meeting involving the Rector Herbert Dale. This building was demolished in 1970 and a new residence taken on in place. Originally thought to be mainly a Victorian building with some seventeenth-century constructions, it was attacked by vandals while empty, revealing a massive timber wall of an early fifteenth-century building. This was removed in two parts to the Passmore Edwards Museum at Stratford. The intention being to return it to a suitable site in Havering which was never found. Unfortunately after many years this superb piece of the Borough's history deteriorated and is no more. Chaplaincy Gardens is a housing development on the site within some of the original boundary walls.

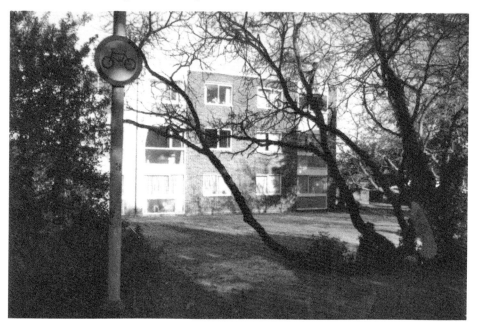

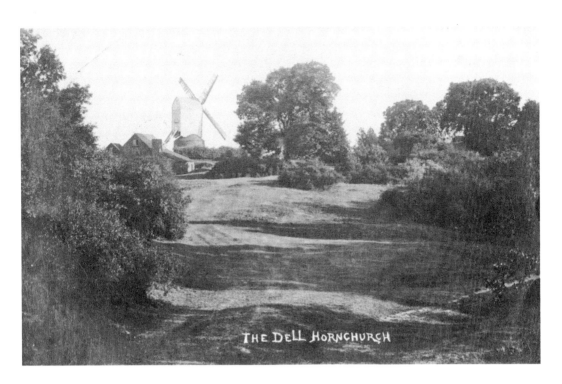

THE DELL HORNCHURCH

Hornchurch Windmill

Hornchurch Windmill and Mill Cottage seen across the Dell in the old photograph. A mill here is recorded as early as 1294 (belonging to the Priory). It is recorded down the centuries – its demise caused by a grass fire on the night of 25 June 1921, when the structure, derelict since 1912 burned furiously. The cottage remains, hidden by the extensive growth of trees and bushes which mercifully hide an electricity station built in the 1960s. A post office van is seen leaving after delivering the mail.

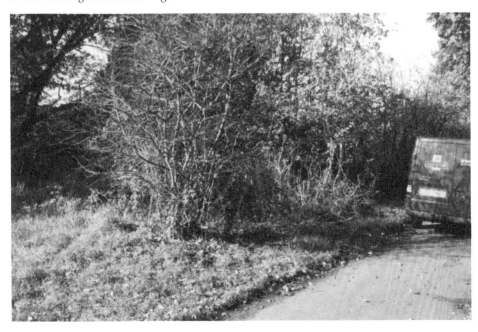

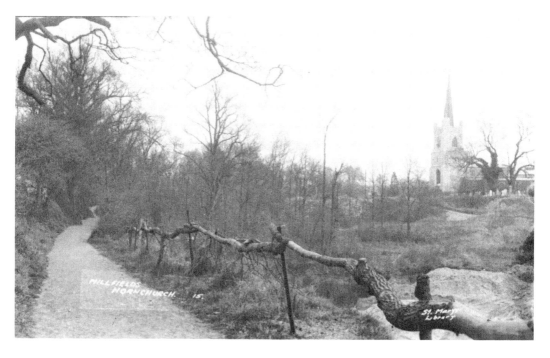

St Andrews Church

A view across the rustic fence over the Dell to St. Andrew's Church in 1930. This play, picnic and recreation area was lost to the local people when it was decided to override local opinion and build an electricity station in the 1960s. Once known as the Millfield, the hollow had been created by mineral workings in a previous era. Today a good view of the church has to be obtained from the path above the Dell on the cemetery side. Here was a linear walking area for monks of the Hornchurch Priory, used for exercise and meditation.

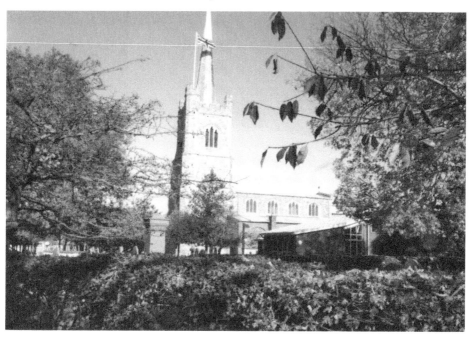

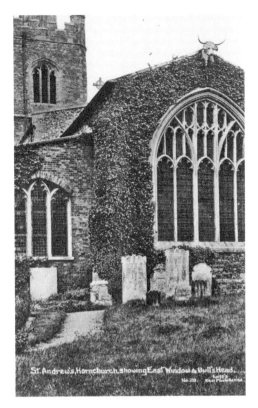

St. Andrew's, Hornchurch, showing East Window & Bull's Head.
No. 20. Real Photo Series

St Andrews Church; East End

The east end of St Andrew's Church about 1920, clearly showing the symbolic bull's head decoration above the east window. Its origins lie in the distant pre-Christian past, later reinforced by the busy market in cattle and leather items evident in the locality in the Middle Ages. Grave markers, some made out of wood, have recorded generations of Hornchurchians laid to rest. The modern view pictures the grassy knoll on the highest ground, 118 feet above sea level. Trinity House once paid for the maintenance of St Andrew's tower, as it was a fixed high point – an aid to shipping navigating the Thames.

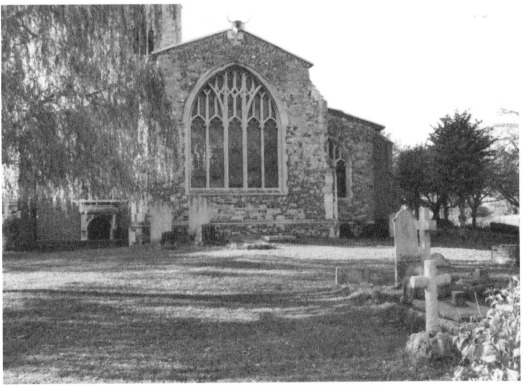

9

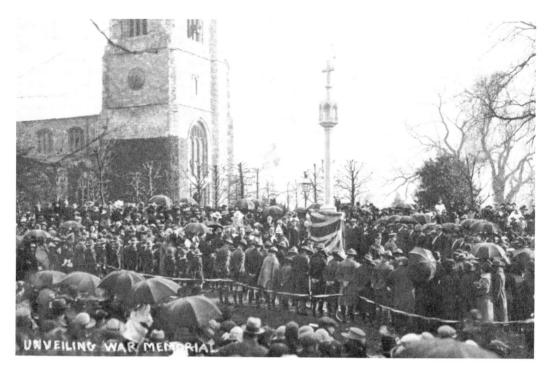

War Memorial

Unveiling the War Memorial in front of St Andrew's after World War I. This attracted a huge crowd in spite of the rain. Notice that most of the spectators are wearing hats – cars were few and far between. The Memorial was the creation of Sir Charles Nicholson, FRIBA, after intense discussion about the best way to remember the dead. In October 2001 the compiler is seen dressed as a Time Lord, with participants in a Time Tour at the War Memorial. Four actors at four historic points portrayed famous people involved in Hornchurch's history, an event devised by the Arts Officer of the London Borough of Havering.

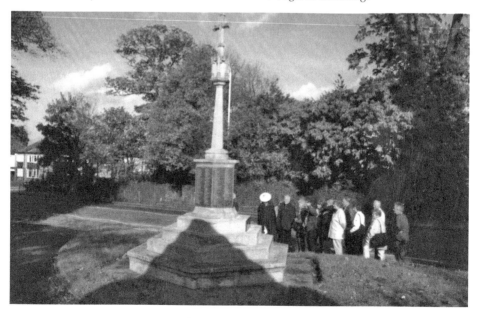

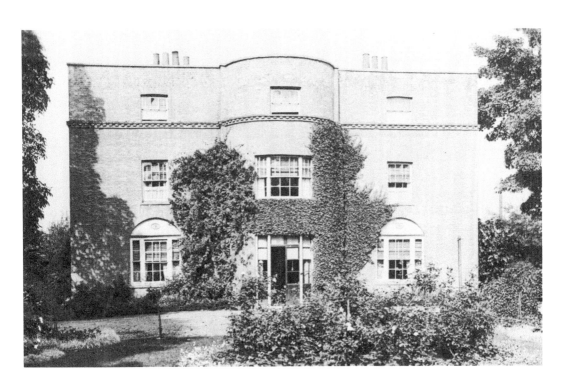

Hornchurch Hall

Hornchurch Hall in the early twentieth century the oldest part had been built in the sixteenth century and it was also partly Victorian. Owned by a succession of families of importance, the manor passed into the ownership of New College when William of Wykeham took over the estates of Hornchurch Priory. One family, the Legats, had existed in the area for three centuries and a half by 1880. The house was seriously damaged in an air raid in 1940 and the remains pulled down in 1947. Today the Robert Beard Youth Centre, named after a local baker and benefactor to the town occupies the site.

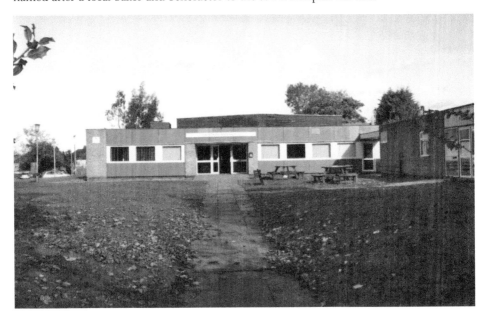

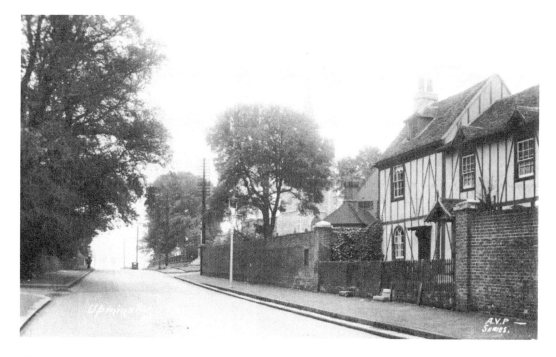

Wykeham Cottage

Wykeham Cottage of the early seventeenth century is one of the remaining older buildings. In the twentieth century it was still two homes – the part on the left being Dale Cottage, until the two cottages were joined together. An earlier churchwarden once lived here and previously it had a connection with the locally significant Ram family. The modern photograph incorporates a parked car, but was taken in a rare moment when no passing traffic obscured the scene. The road normally carrying a continuous stream of every type of vehicle – cars, buses and lorries.

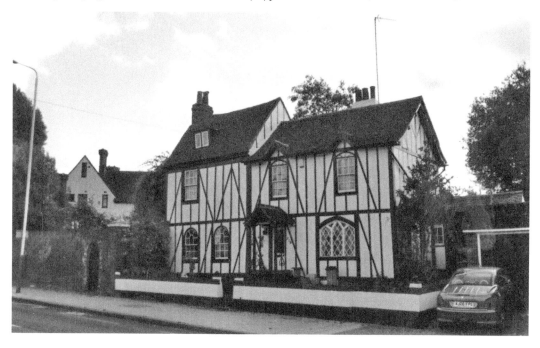

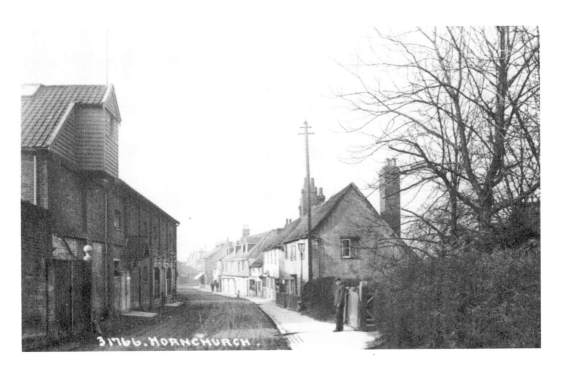

High Street

Showing the section of the High Street then known as Church Street, in about 1912. The office frontage of Hornchurch Brewery stands in shadow on the left, with reflections from the other side of the street in its windows. The buildings on the right once formed a continuous line from round the corner at the bottom end. The modern photograph shows the gaps which have since appeared. A car park in the recent photograph has appeared in place of the cottages on the near right hand side. But the right hand side of the hill today displays perhaps the best remaining group of old buildings in the town.

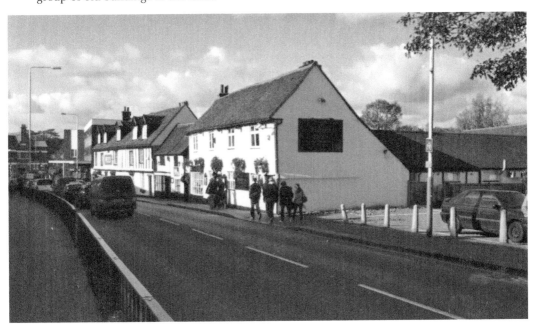

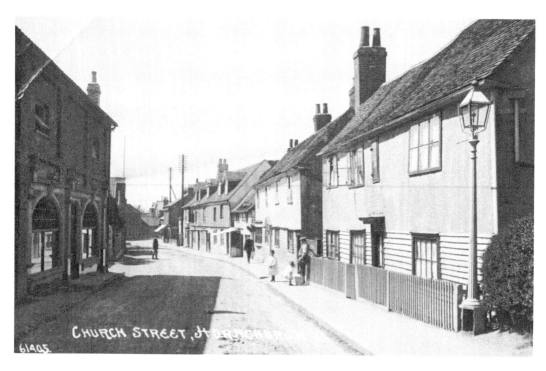

CHURCH STREET, H...
61905

High Street and Brewery

A similar view in the old photograph shows the towering wooden superstructure of the brewery premises by the gateway. In the modern view we see how the line of shops with flats above has been set back.

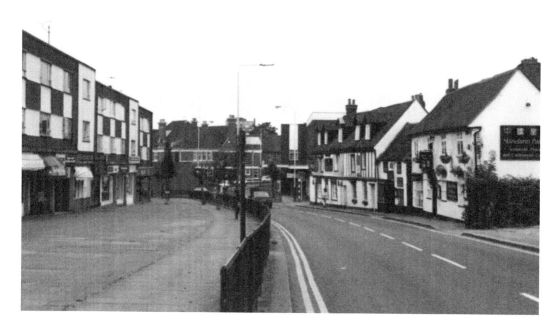

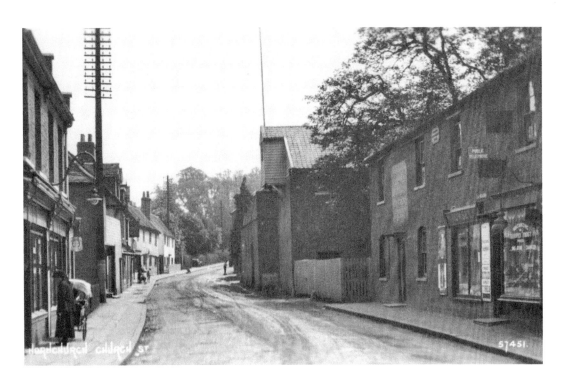

King's Head

Looking back up the hill in this photograph published as a postcard by Battrams of the Post Office in Station Road, the continuous and sinuous line of Church Street can be seen with the brewery above and the old shops below facing the Kings Head Inn and old buildings on the left. Rumsey's famous cycle shop premises are at bottom right by the corner of Station Road. The new photograph shows the modern line of shops set back on the left and the ceaseless line of vehicles feeding down the hill on the right.

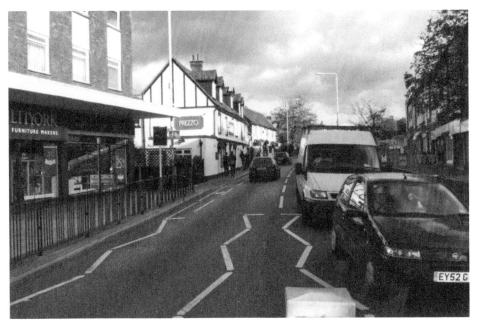

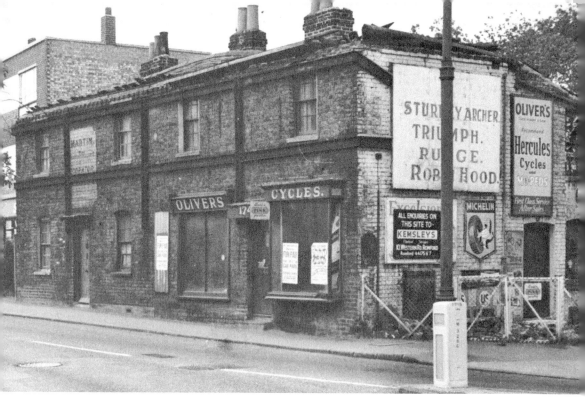

Rumsey's Corner

Just before the demolition of Rumsey's Corner this photograph captures new buildings beyond on the left. A line of shops with flats above fills what had been a vacant lot for a number of years after the brewery was demolished. Oliver's Cycles had taken over Rumsey's in a persistence of the same trade, also seen at the other end of Hornchurch High Street. Raymond Rumsey had died in 1952. The new shopping parade houses a wide variety of occupations and trades.

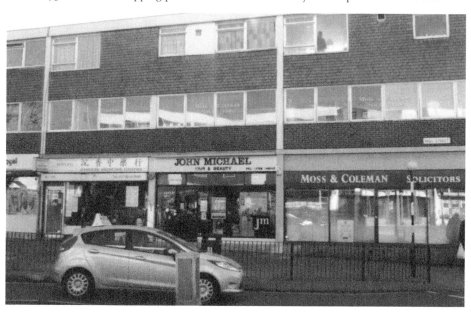

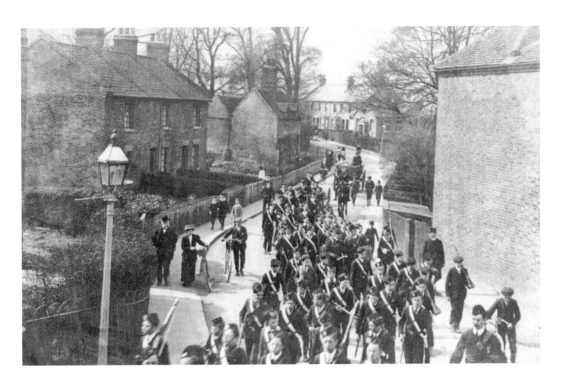

Station Road

The Church Lads Brigade march out of Station Road at the back of the White Hart in 1909. At this time there was no exit from the lane on the southern side of the White Hart, apart from a narrow footpath. In the modern view we can glimpse how the cottages on the left later had shops built over the front gardens. The houses on the right seen in the old view are gone and traffic now complies with the one way circular system.

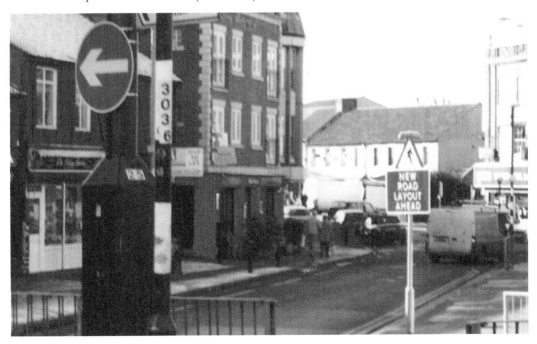

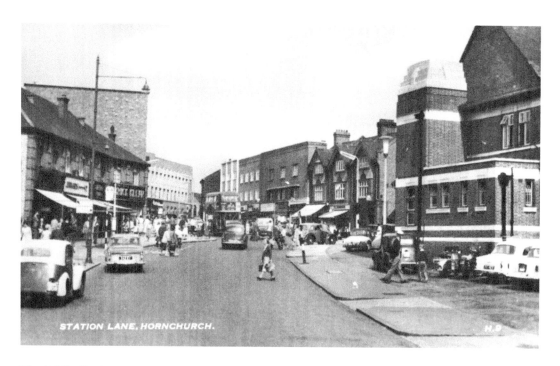

STATION LANE, HORNCHURCH.

The White Hart

In the 1950s the one way system is in force though at a gentler pace than now. Cars almost amble about and some are parked by the White Hart, which had been rebuilt in 1935 replacing an 1872 building, which itself had replaced a really ancient hostelry. Today we see the White Hart recently redeveloped as several units with ASK Restaurant on the south side. Beyond on the left Free's card and gift shop has survived for many years amidst the constantly changing fascias along the High Street generally.

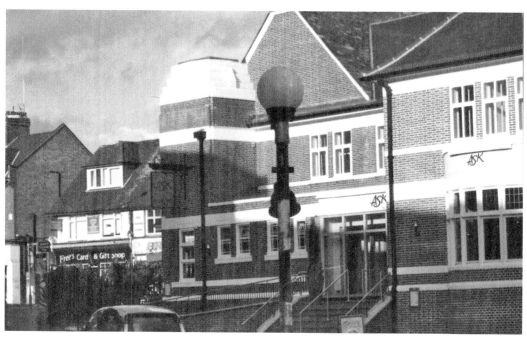

163 High Street

Hayward and Co – Estate Agents at 163 High Street Hornchurch in October 1931 – with the proprietor (?) standing outside. The house adverts are Spartan and rather boring compared to today's window displays – no photographs can be seen. A three figure telephone number – Hornchurch 294 was assigned to the premises. Today 163 High Street appears on the extreme right of the Parade and has recently hosted a tanning shop.

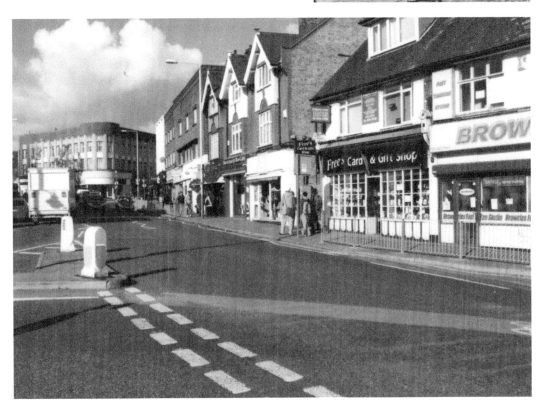

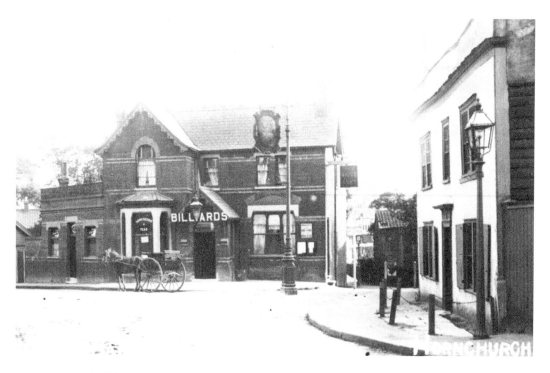

White Hart Rebuild

The 1872 rebuild of the White Hart constructed after a fire destroyed a centuries old hostelry is seen here about 1908. Beyond the Chain House on the right a narrow footpath descends to Station Road. Today the successor building now a multiply occupied centre of dining/leisure activities is very obviously on an island site. A road constructed over the footpath in the late 1920s has resulted in a one way system rotating around the 1935 building which has been refurbished.

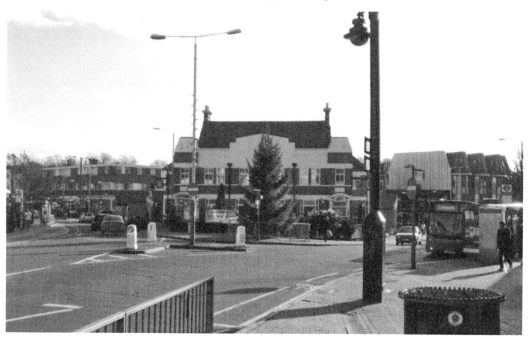

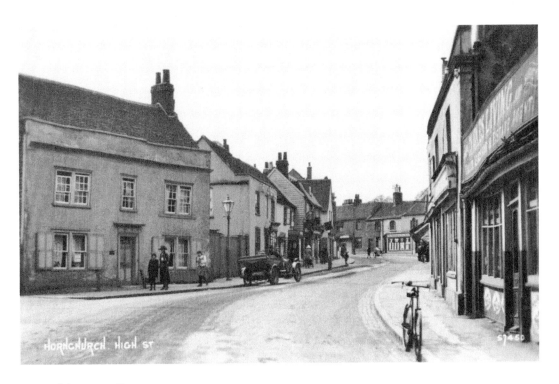

High Street Changes

An early motor car waits in the High Street in about 1920 by the buildings that include Aley's the bakers on the left. This block was later demolished to widen the roadway and pavement. Charles Living at 165 on the right trades from rather ramshackle looking premises. A view round the right hand side of the White Hart block shows how the widening of the High Street in the second half of the twentieth century has been swamped by the increasing traffic passing through.

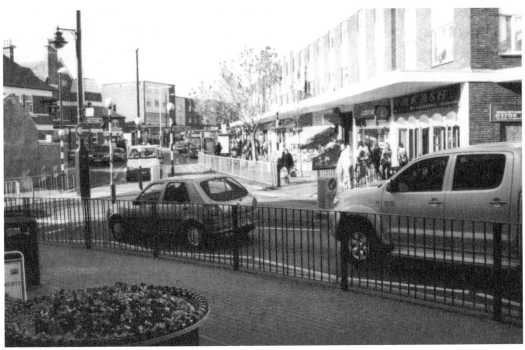

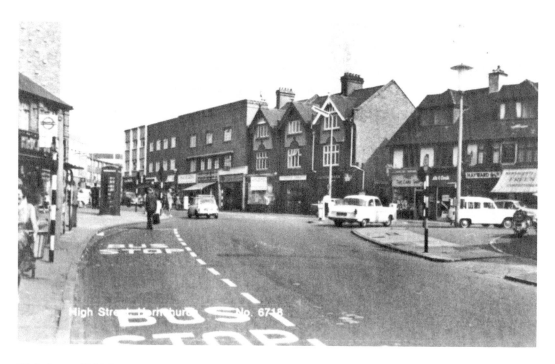

High Street Vehicles

In the early 1960s the High Street had acquired a bus stop lane, the forerunner of further road markings that are not particularly photogenic. The motor cars in the one way system are rather boxy in shape compared to today's streamlined vehicles. The modern roadway has acquired more painted lines and instructions. Otherwise the building line has not altered to any extent over forty-fifty years.

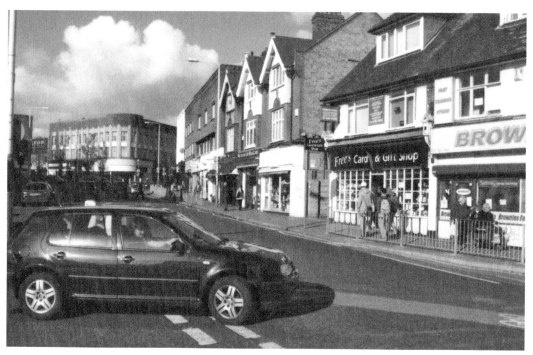

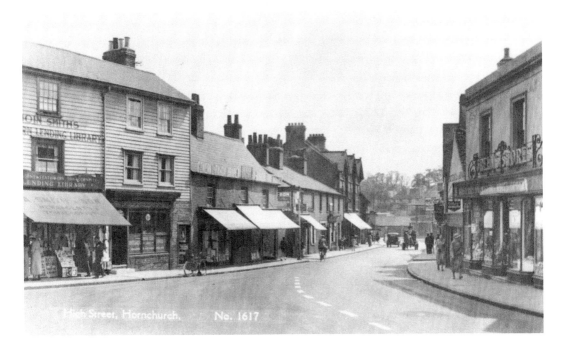

North Street Junction

Looking round the High Street corner at the junction of North Street (branching away on the left), just a portion of the White Hart can be seen. About 1929 the timber faced buildings on the left, now replaced including A. Smith's lending library, newsagents and tobacconists and W. Franklyn's high-class cobblers. The right hand side includes the ubiquitous Green's stores selling groceries, provisions, wines and spirits. Two bicycles, many pedestrians, one car and a horse and cart make up the action. The first public library in Hornchurch did not open until 7 September 1936. Today the pace has increased and High Street is a busy traffic artery.

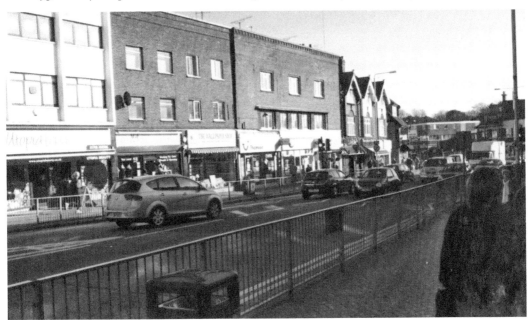

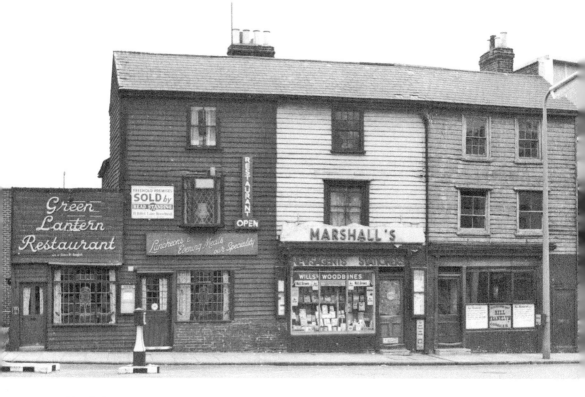

North Street

A frontal view of the last of the weather-boarded buildings leading into North Street in the 1960s. Smith's has become Marshall's with an added fascia suggesting a 1950s origin. The Green Lantern building and perhaps the whole block has been sold. The building line will be set back to the line seen at the right allowing more pavement space. The resulting frontages can be seen in the modern photograph.

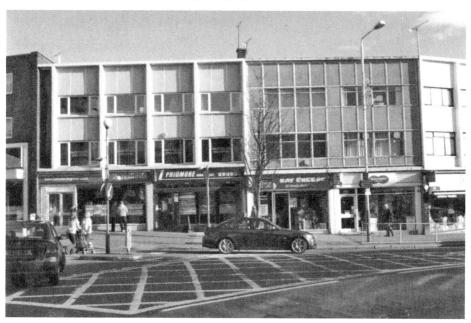

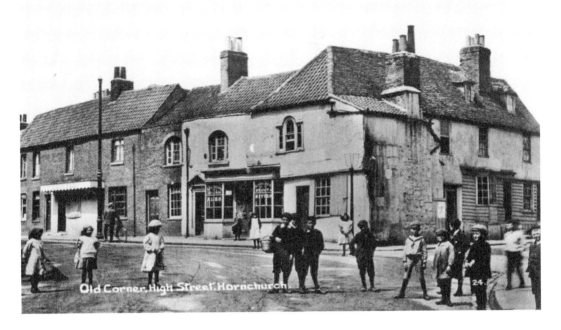

Old Corner

In 1912 if you look at the left hand corner of the Britannia building, once an inn, a substantial rag-stone construction to the chimney fronting on North Street can be seen. It is believed that this was once a hostelry for travellers and pilgrims run by the Hornchurch Priory. Looking at this corner today Burton's menswear and Dorothy Perkins ladies fashions occupies the site which was rebuilt just before the outbreak of World War II.

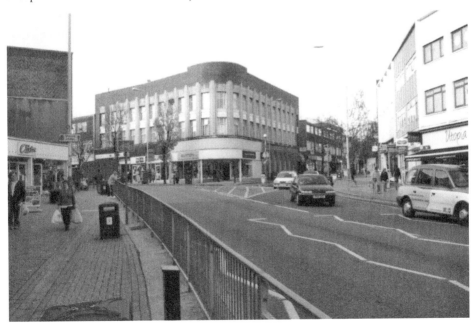

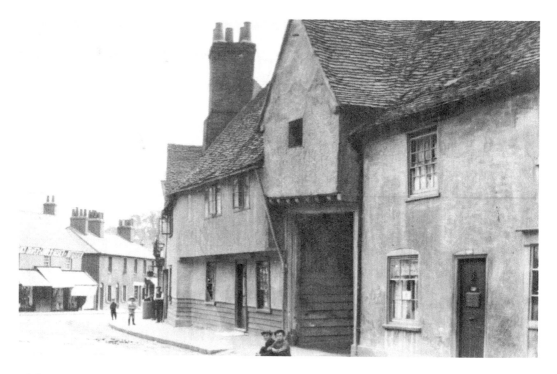

High Street West

At the beginning of the westward section of the High Street opposite the Britannia in the early twentieth century a charming and ancient building also formerly an inn was still standing. It is recorded that a highwayman pursued by the law was sheltered by his mother in one of the myriad buildings formerly the stable block around the yard in earlier times. A different story today with a bank building, surprisingly not set back, next to a bakers and café which has been rebuilt behind the new building line next door.

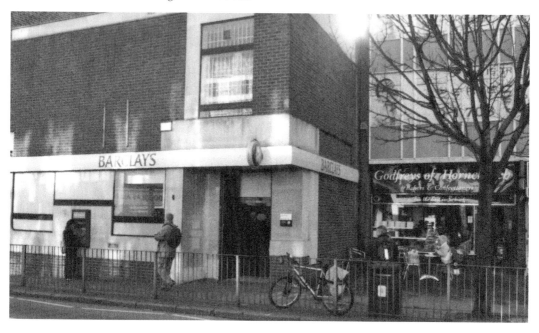

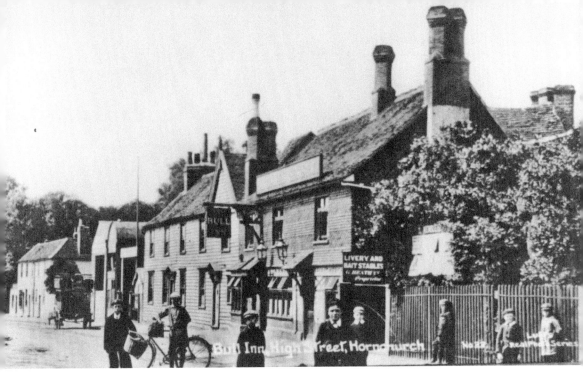

The Bull Inn

The Bull Inn and the old frontage with a strange omnibus type vehicle beyond advertises its livery and bait stables in about 1910. The whole frontage towards Billet Lane can be seen. Today the area to the right of the altered sixteenth-century structure has been opened out. Bollards protect a modern courtyard space suitable for open air dining in the better weather. The east end of a large Sainsbury's store crowds into the picture at left.

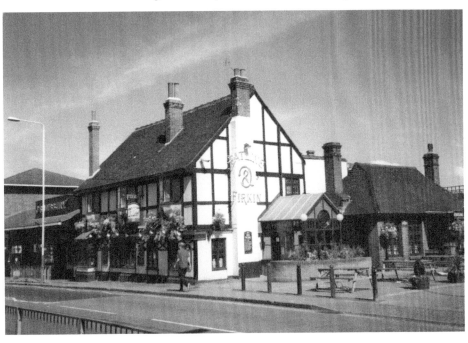

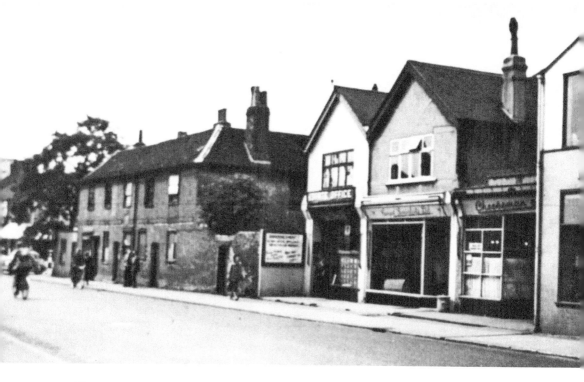

Billet Lane Corner

Beyond the Bull in about 1960 shops and cottages are seen with a row of almshouses on the corner of Billet Lane. These were soon to be demolished leaving an open space fronted by a large billboard. The site eventually proved tempting to developers. In recent times at Christmas Sainsbury's store has filled the entire block on the right complementing a busier shopping area opposite and beyond.

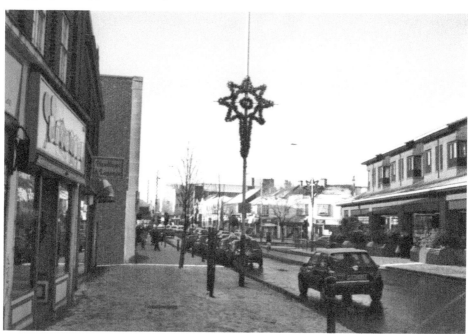

Billet Lane Shops

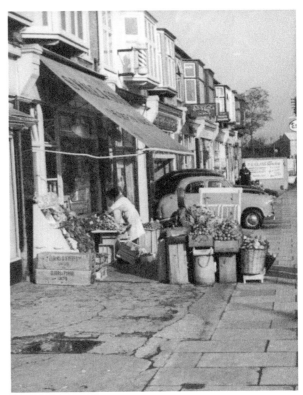

Looking up Billet Lane in the late 1950s the shops included a greengrocer's, a barber's, an estate agents, a glass service and a garage. The hard winter of 1947 has probably left damage to the concrete in front of the shops. In the distance are the fire station and firemen's houses on the other side of the road. In modern times the line of retail businesses includes a lighting shop, a florists and new housing, with the Queen's Theatre rising in the distance, and Sainsbury's and its car park on the right hand side.

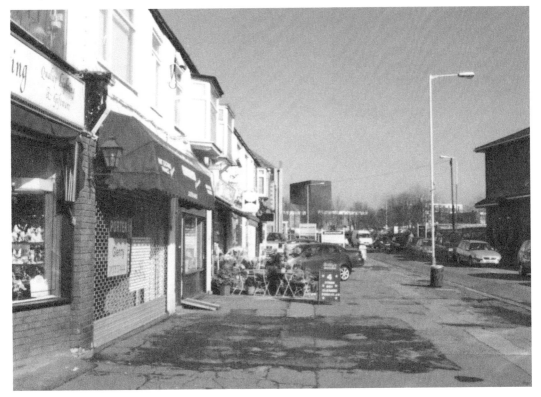

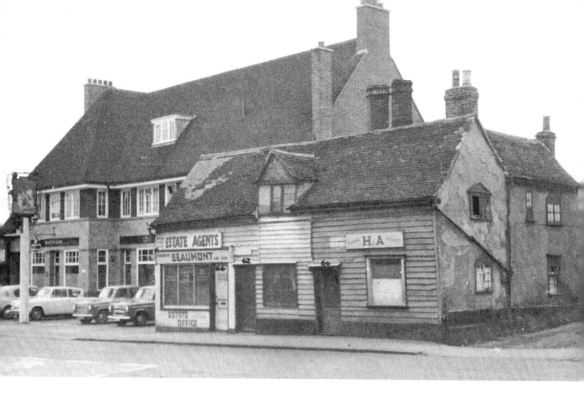

Cricketers

The rebuilt Cricketers public house in about 1960 with some remaining earlier buildings at 60-64 High Street. These were many centuries old, as was the original Cricketers, probably named after Hornchurch's all conquering cricket team of the early nineteenth century which was unbeaten for several years and attracted a fashionable following of the sporting fancy. A refurbished Cricketers announces it is catering to the modern taste with "live music and sports throughout the week". To the right is a new block containing bars and restaurants.

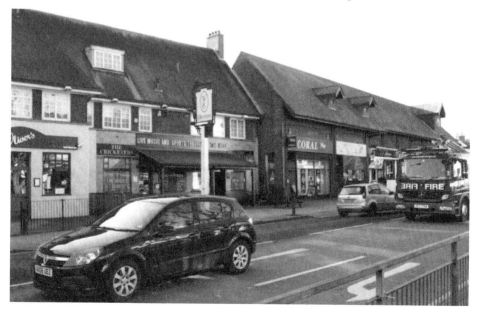

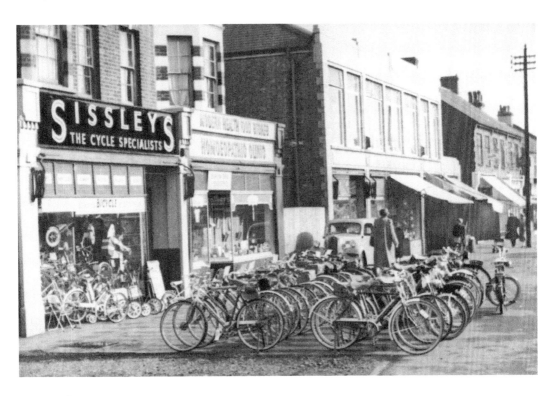

Cycles

The shops along the cinema end of the High Street included in the 1950s Sissley's the cycle specialists. Classic Chassis now cater for a changed style of biking in the twenty-first century.

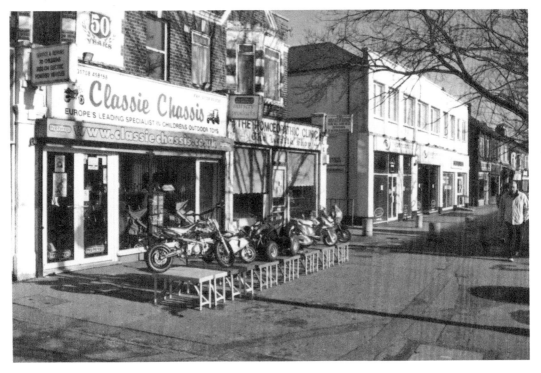

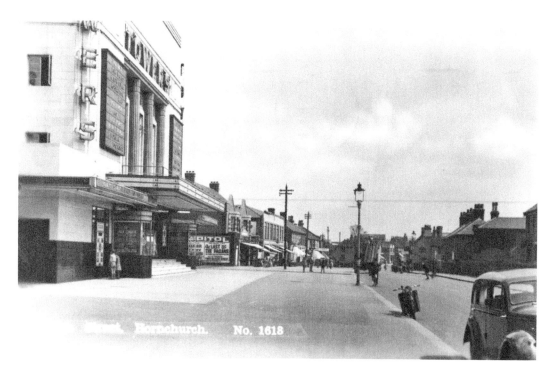

Towers Cinema

The Towers Cinema opened on 3 August 1935 at 31 High Street. It was designed by the specialist architects Kemp and Tasker. In its early years before World War II it would cater in the evenings to a large audience in pre-television days for the masses. Outside in the quiet of the afternoon a car and a motor bike are parked facing the wrong way. Today a vehicle is parked on the pavement outside what was once a candy shop serving the cinema. The main premises are now a bingo hall.

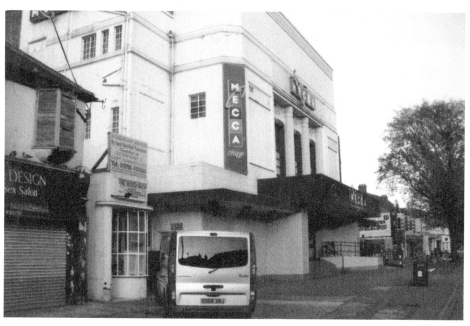

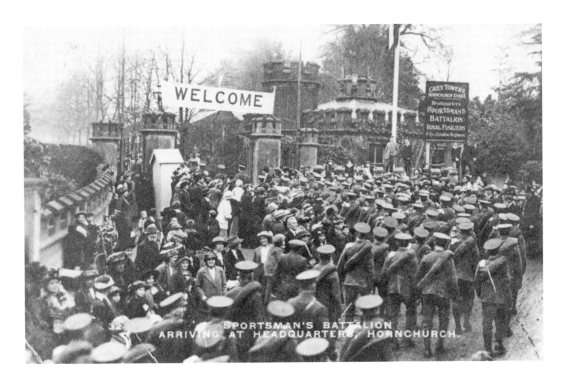

Grey Towers

The Sportsman's Battalion are seen here arriving at the lodge gates of the house and estate of Grey Towers, pressed into service as a World War I holding camp and HQ. Many local ladies and children have come to watch. One of the military units which were to wake up the social life of a sleepy village. Today the lodges have gone – Grey Towers Avenue housing built after the war lines the avenue, and a footpath leads across a green space.

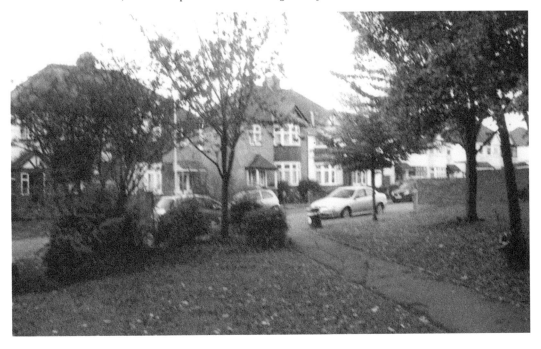

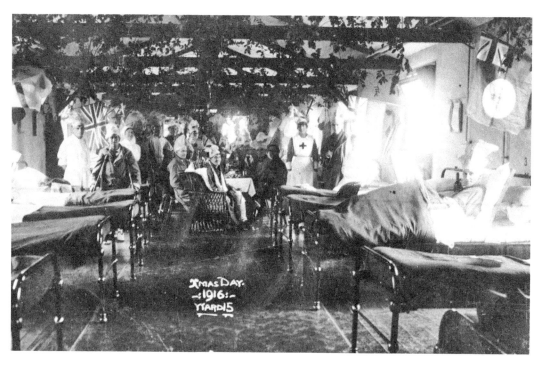

Ward 15

When the Sportsmen had departed for France the Grey Towers estate was taken over as a base camp and hospital for injured New Zealanders. Ward 15 is shown at Christmas 1916. The nurses and soldiers are attempting to get into the spirit of the season. A recent view shows the grounds of the former Grey Towers housing an allotment.

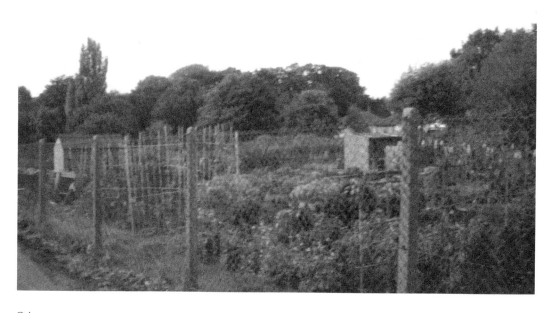

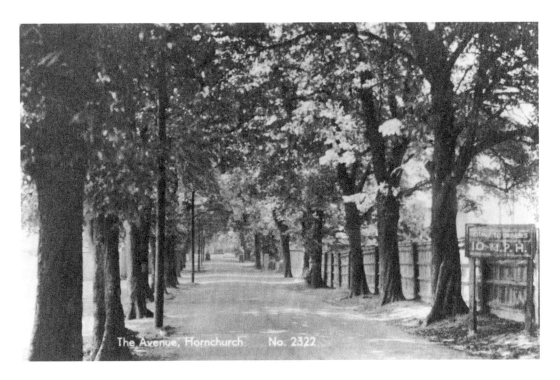

The Avenue, Hornchurch   No. 2322

Harrow Lodge

The avenue at the entrance to Harrow Lodge about 1930. A warning notice to drivers gives the speed limit as 10 miles per hour. The lodge was built in 1787, a stuccoed two-storey building. It was damaged twice, once in 1858 by fire, and again in 1944 by flying bomb. It once sat at the front of the farmlands on the Harrow Lodge estate. The building became the first and main branch library of the area in 1936. Harrow Lodge is now a park and each year the Havering Show is held in the grounds. A swimming pool, opened in 1956, close to the house has grown into a larger leisure centre, increasing the flow of traffic along the avenue.

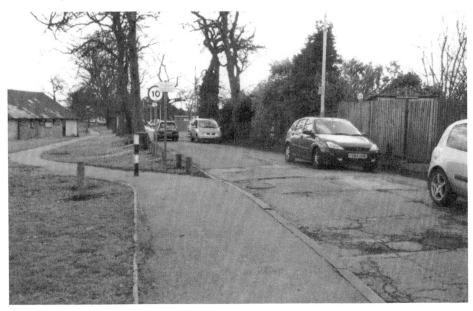

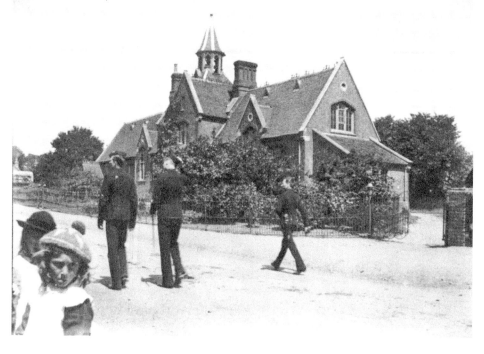

Hornchurch School

Hornchurch Village School, built in the nineteenth century, is partly obscured by bushes in this photograph, probably taken by plate camera in the early 1900s. Three members of the Church Lads Brigade are passing by with two young ladies in their Sunday best watching the photographer at work in North Street. The old school replaced by a new one in Westland Avenue beyond has been redesigned as a christian centre and has lost its belltower since the original picture. Pioneer House looms on the corner beyond.

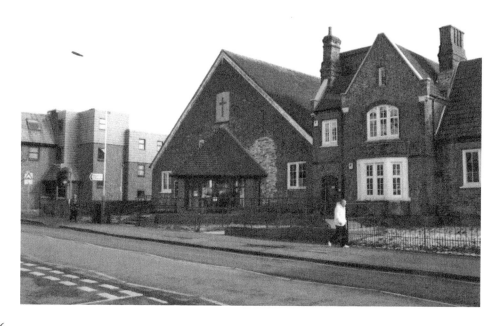

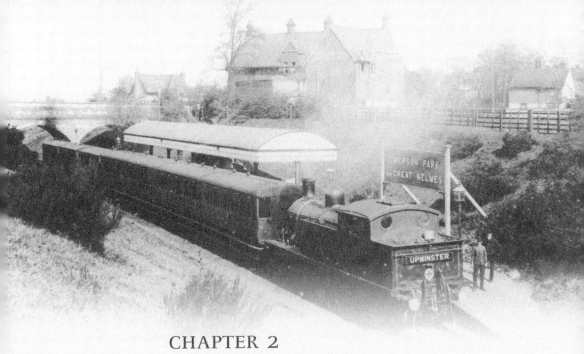

CHAPTER 2

Wheels

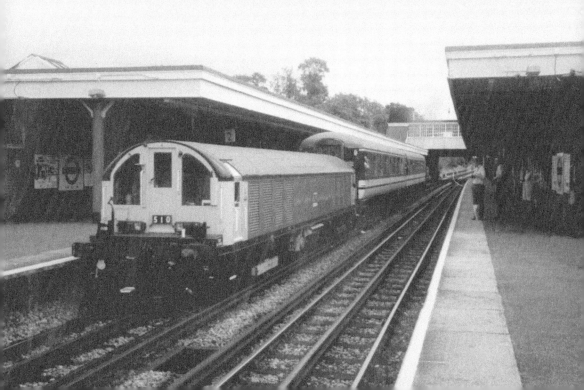

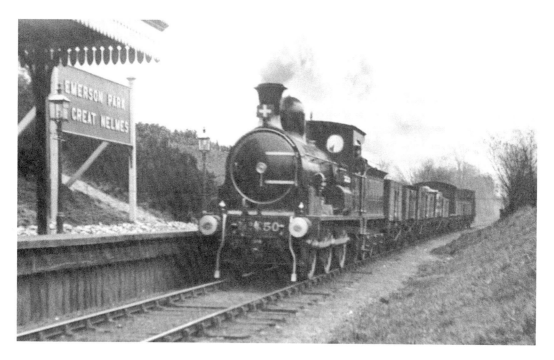

Trains

A freight train passes through Emerson Park on an early working. Today an electric service leaves bound similarly for Romford. Quite a lot of vegetation has grown up on the cuttings – a refuge for wildlife. The line has survived innumerable closure threats since the poorly researched report by so called businessman Dr Beeching ignored a long term future of roads full of traffic. This branch line takes just 8 minutes between Upminster and Romford – unbeatable by road.

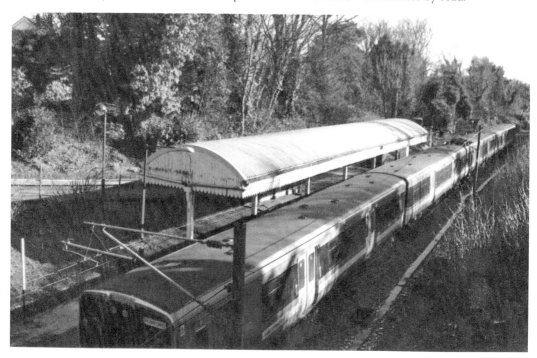

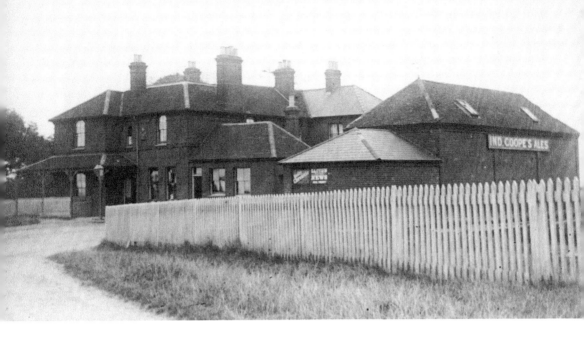

Hornchurch Station

Truly a country station yet the buildings bulk large – the Hornchurch train station about 1912. The structure includes staff and passenger quarters and refreshment facilities. It took quite a number of years to have an effect on housing and population growth in the area. The real spur to this was the augmentation of local services to Fenchurch Street by the extension of the District Line to Upminster and electrification. Many of the commuters today, as can be seen, will transfer to a car at the end of the journey for the final leg home. But there are useful bus services connecting areas between Romford and Hornchurch.

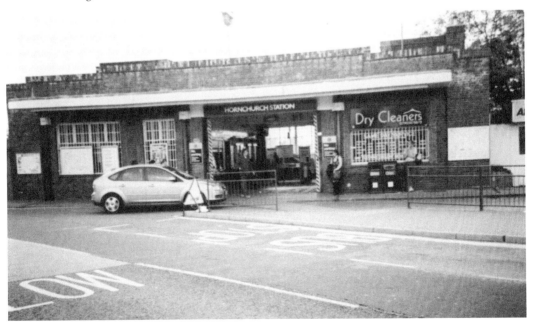

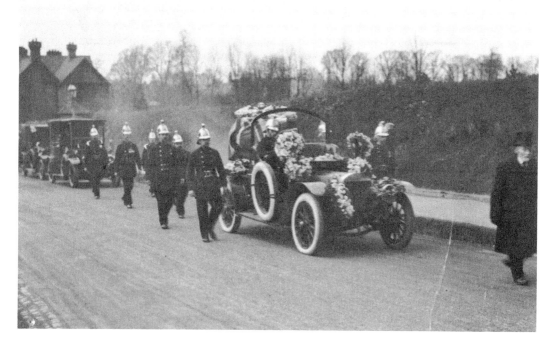

Funerals Through Time

An early twentieth-century motorised funeral procession involving a local fireman, whose colleagues accompany the cortege to the local cemetery. In late 2009 a funeral procession temporarily halts on its way down Upminster Road. Homes built through most of the decades of the twentieth century line the former country lane.

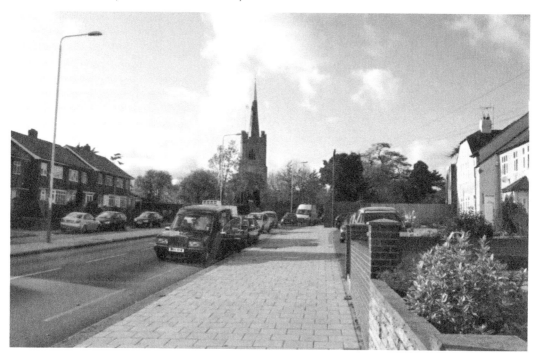

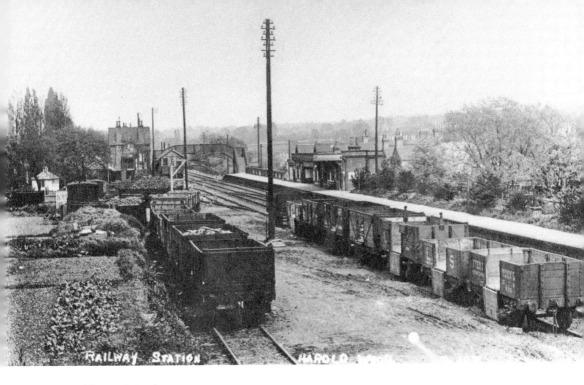

Harold Wood Station

The goods yard at Harold Wood station about 1925. Used by the local industries such as the brickworks and Matthew's Seed Merchants and Agriculturalists. Much coal was also transported by rail, being at the time the principal heating medium for houses everywhere. On the far platform are the remains of the original station and farther down the former footbridge and signal box. Behind this lay the staggered 'down' platform. The yard has now been converted into a car park, and the down platform now faces the up version.

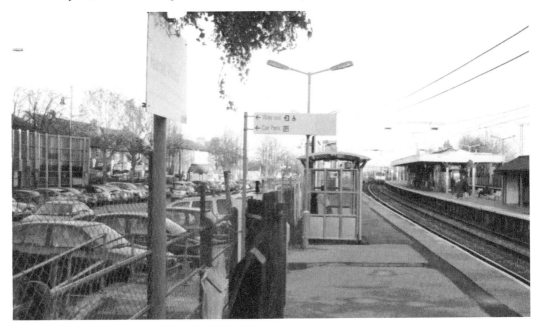

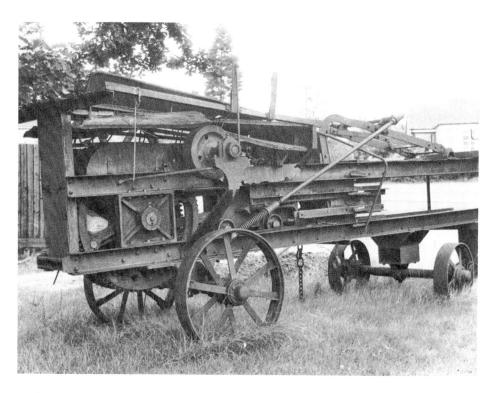

Agricultural Machinery

A magnificent piece of old agricultural machinery which remained at Bretons Farm after farming operations ceased. On a visit I chose smaller farming implements such as ploughs to include in the nostalgia display at the Tithe Barn in Upminster. Mechanised haymaking at a local farm, possibly Lilyputts in the 1950s is seen in the later photograph. This farm, incidentally, continued to use horses long after many farmers had abandoned horse working.

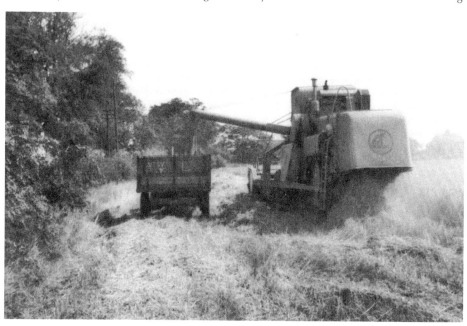

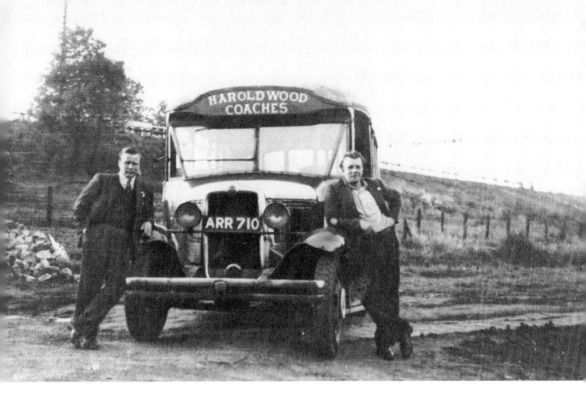

Coaches

The Leach brothers who set up Harold Wood Coaches in a golden age of popular public transport. The firm continued as a family business until recent times. In 2010 many coaches from outside the borough travelled along local roads, as in this picture of Hornchurch Road.

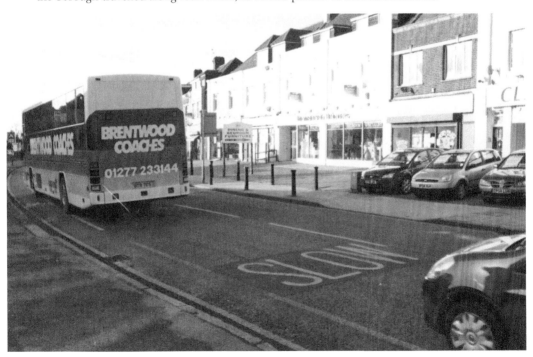

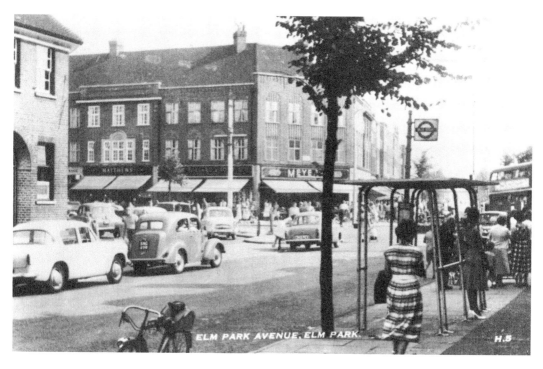

Elm Park Avenue

Elm Park Avenue in the late '50s and early '60s, like other areas was beginning to experience an increase in motor cars and traffic generally. The scene, rather sedate to modern eyes, includes potential customers for the 252 bus, while a 165 turns right in the distance. The cars of the time are parked anywhere without special controls. The larger vehicles of today spend more time on the move, as here in Hornchurch Road.

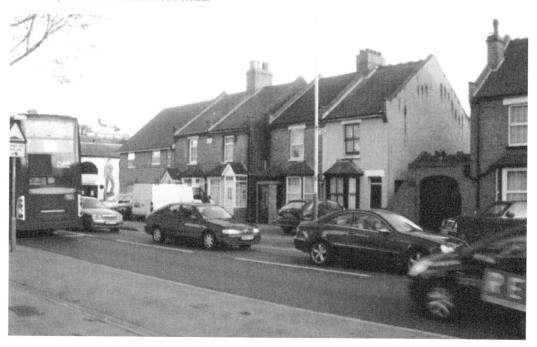

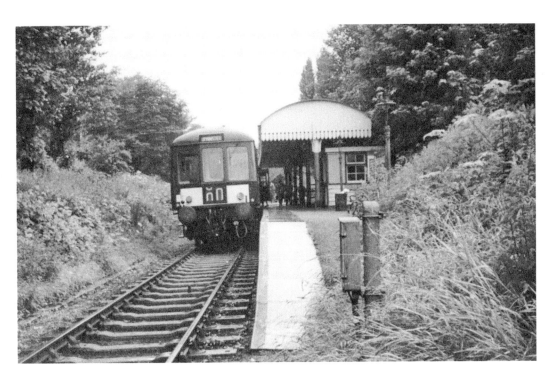

Emerson Park Station

A diesel unit in Emerson Park station in 1963. Having resisted many attempts at closure the line was surprisingly electrified when diesels were taken out of service. Passengers waiting for a train stare out at the verdant slopes, making it appear this location could be miles from anywhere.

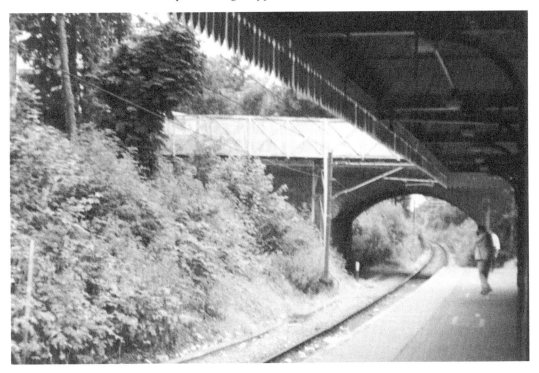

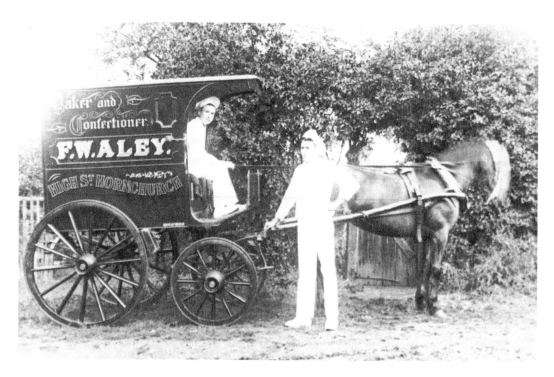

Wheels

Wheels of a former time. F. W. Aley's baker's van in daily use in Edwardian Hornchurch is here waiting to take part in an early Hornchurch Carnival against a rural setting common throughout Hornchurch at the time. In Elm Park Avenue today improved pavements lend a very metropolitan air to the picture, as buses, cars and delivery vehicles try to keep to their schedule, against a background of shops and shoppers.

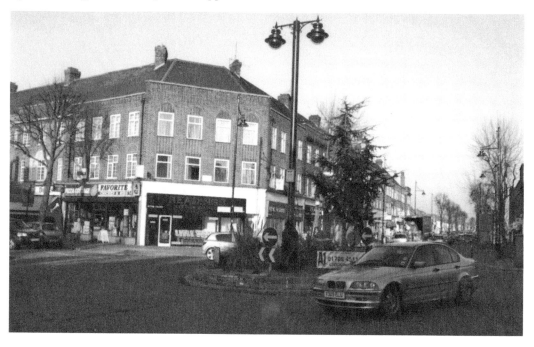

46

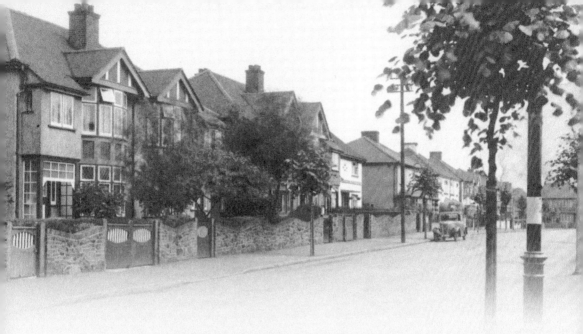

CHAPTER 3
North and West

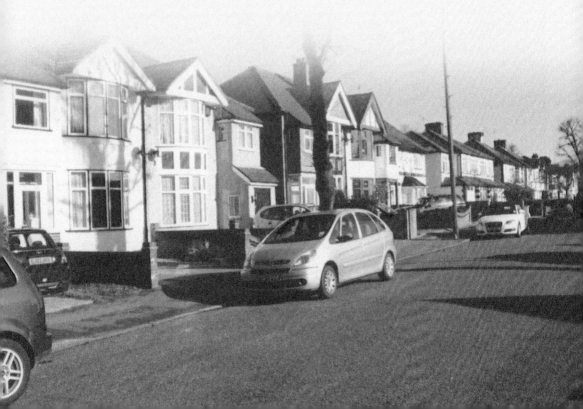

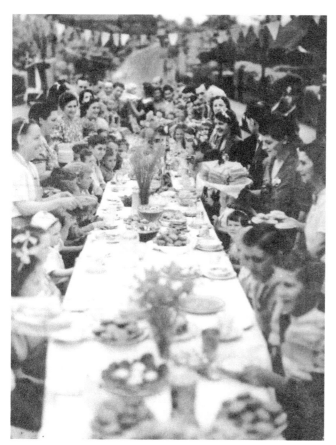

Celebrations

A street party to celebrate the end of World War II is in full swing along Hillview Avenue. Among the youngsters seated at the table with parents and family standing behind, halfway along is a young dark haired Leslie Parker, who has managed to get his whole profile into shot on the left just beyond the vase of artificial (?) flowers. In spite of rationing, sandwiches and cakes abound. In contrast, a party involved in the Time Tour event celebrating Hornchurch's long history, a group of more mature people tours Langtons Gardens, with the owner portrayed by actor John Halstead.

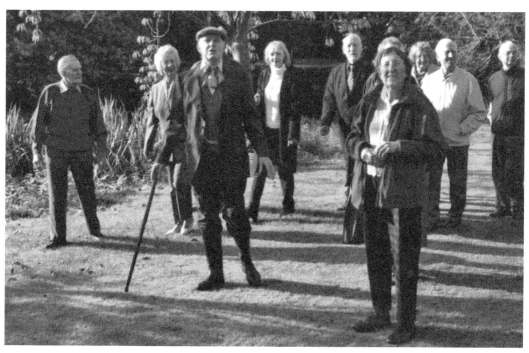

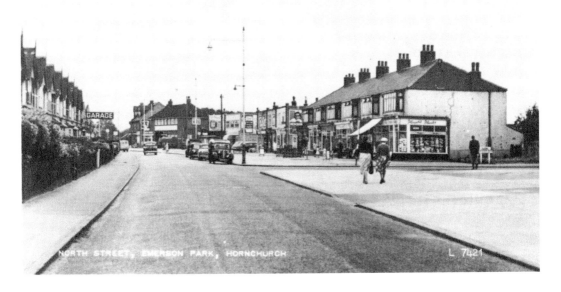

North Street, Looking Up

A view up North Street in the 1950s. Notice how tidy the street and pavements are. In this era there were not so many disposable wrappings or consumption of food and drink outside the home. In the far distance is the milk depot where the road curves left. Today larger vehicles are parked closer to the commercial enterprises on the right.

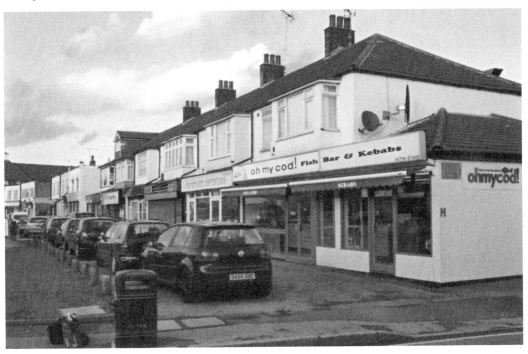

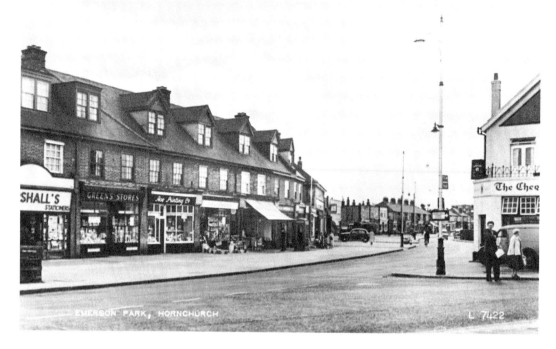

North Street, Looking Down

Looking back down North Street from the Chequers public house intersection we get a good view of the shops above the bend. These include a stationers, grocers (Green's Stores) and ironmongers. Many more people are on foot compared with today. A sign directs people to Hornchurch Council Offices. Today's view includes different types of businesses, and beyond the car in the right distance, new housing is built where the milk distribution depot once stood.

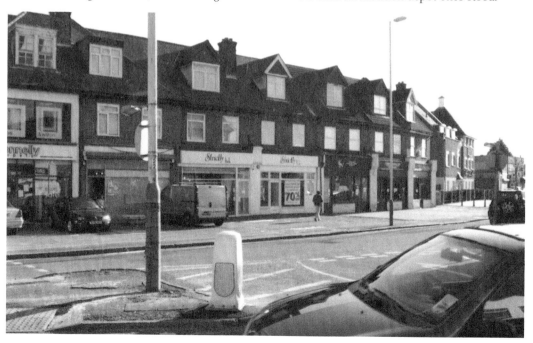

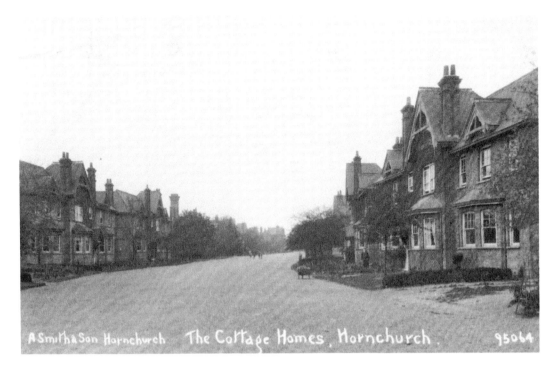

The Cottage Homes, Hornchurch

The Cottage Homes

In 1928 Hornchurch Cottage Homes, originally set up by St Leonard's Shoreditch parish to accommodate workhouse children away from bad inner city influences can be seen to occupy a large area- the whole site covered eighty-six acres with a farm, eleven large cottages, probationary lodge, infirmary, schools, baths and workshops. In 2010 the area has been developed as a housing estate – St Leonard's Hamlet, incorporating a few of the original buildings, such as the probationary lodge.

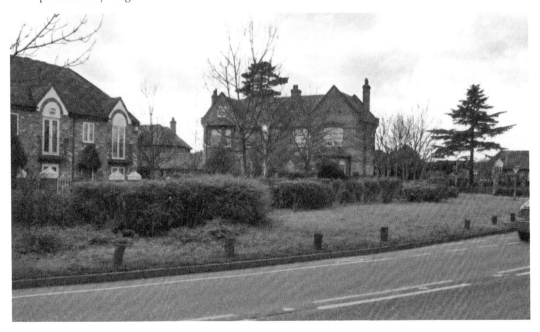

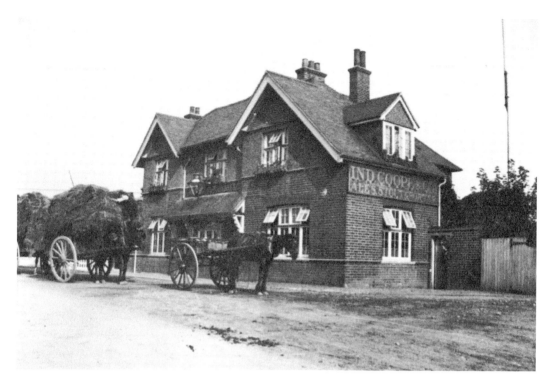

The Harrow Inn

Judging by the cart outside the Harrow Inn, seen not long after its 1894 rebuild, it could justifiably be named 'A Load of Hay'. It had been the resort of local agricultural workers and passing travellers. Farm wagons stopped here on their way to market. Today the Harrow has become a popular eating place with gardens for alfresco dining.

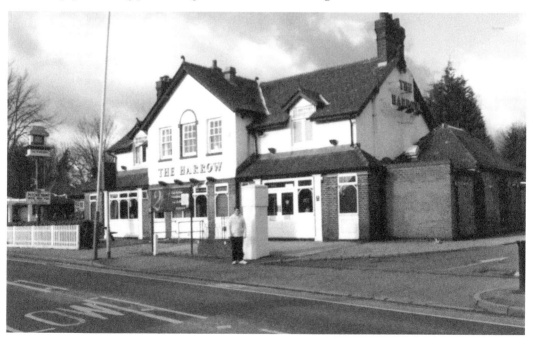

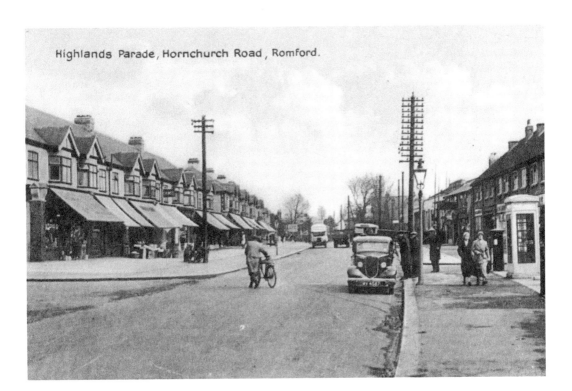

Highlands Parade, Hornchurch Road, Romford.

Highlands Parade

Hornchurch in the vicinity of Hylands Parade in the 1930s. Telegraph poles still line the road, and there is a nice example of the light coloured version of the standard telephone kiosk. A bus stands outside the Hornchurch Garage, opened in July 1924, and originally called Romford Garage. A changed scene, minus the closed bus garage, now housing and well trafficked, is filled with modern businesses.

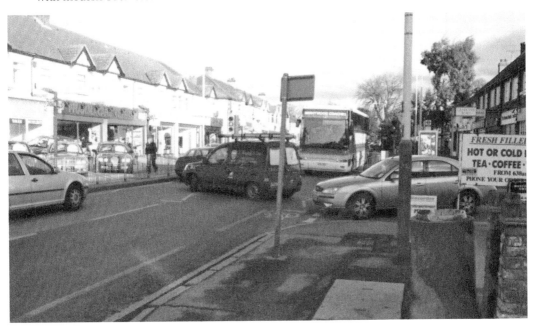

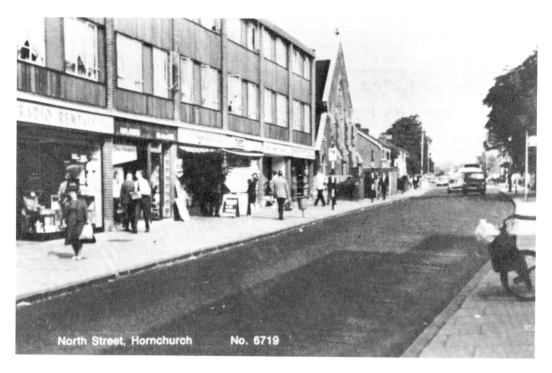

North Street, Hornchurch   No. 6719

North Street

North Street leads away from the High Street in a typical scene from the 1960s. Radio Rentals where you could also rent a television and other shops form an extension to High Street trading. The chapel on the west side has been rebuilt as an Iceland store with the church premises above, and the cottages above in the distance have been demolished and a 1960s building set back from the road.

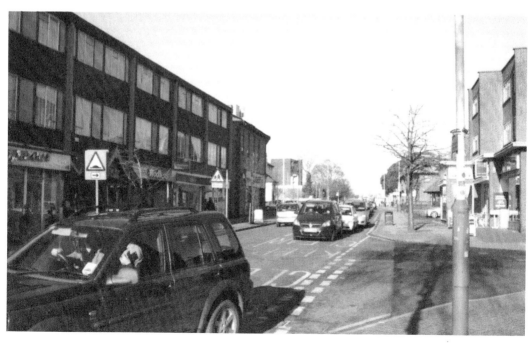

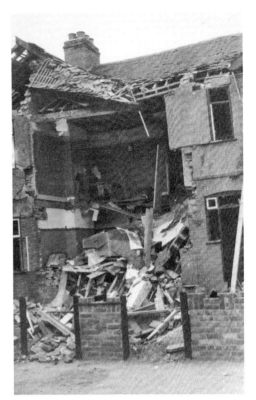

Park Lane

This house in Park Lane towards the northwest of Hornchurch received a devastating hit by High Explosive Bomb on 24 August 1940, when World War II came home to Britain. The first attempt to evacuate children away from Hornchurch had met with apathy. Out of 3,000 forms sent to parents, 60 were returned and only 10 stated a willingness to evacuate. The scene today.

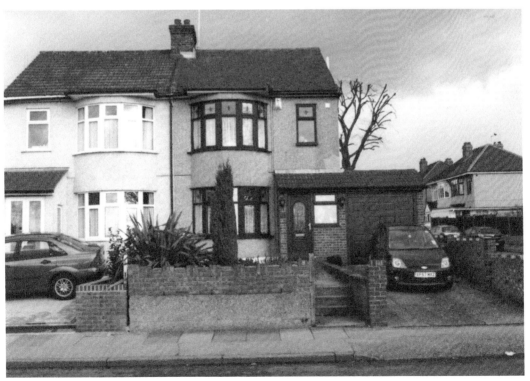

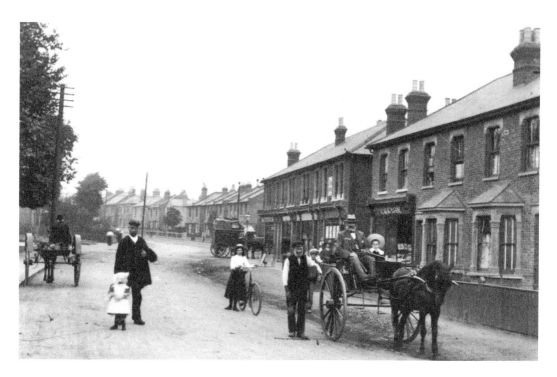

Brentwood Road

An assortment of old time vehicles at the northwest extremity of the former Hornchurch Urban District. Part of Brentwood Road is seen about 1910, the junction with Park Lane is in the background. Most of the properties pictured still exist, but house fronts have become shop fronts, as can be seen in the current photograph. The smart pony and trap is probably occupied by Mr Mason, the shopkeeper. The building line up Brentwood Road on the east is almost unaltered.

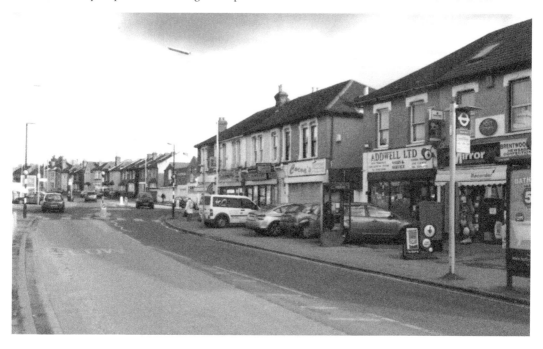

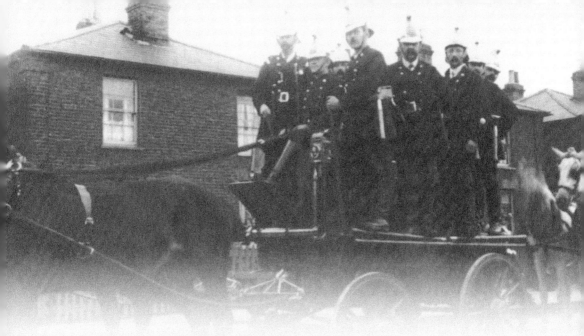

CHAPTER 4

Changing Times

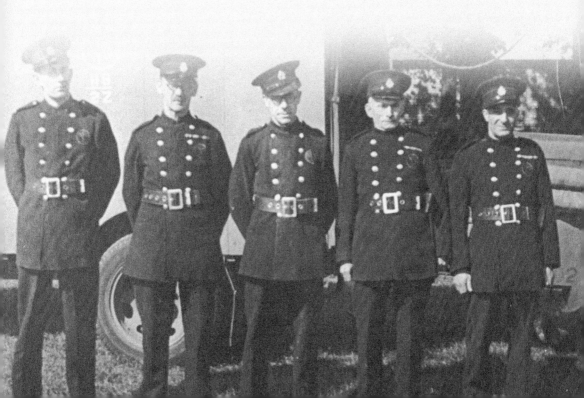

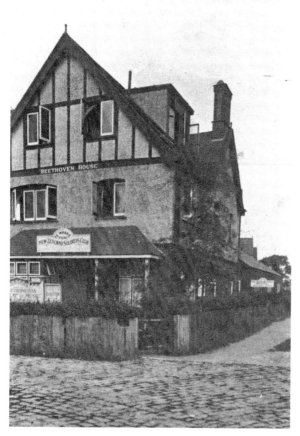

Beethoven House

Beethoven House in Butts Green Road, at the end of World War I, is in transition. It bears a notice with the name "Te Whare Puni" and the explanation "New Zealand's Soldiers Club" as it had been dedicated as a rest and recreation facility for wounded troops from the Grey Towers hospital site. At the rear is a notice "Soldiers only". However, a new use on the ground floor is indicated – The Metropolitan Academy of Music. The house remains in 2010 as commercial premises.

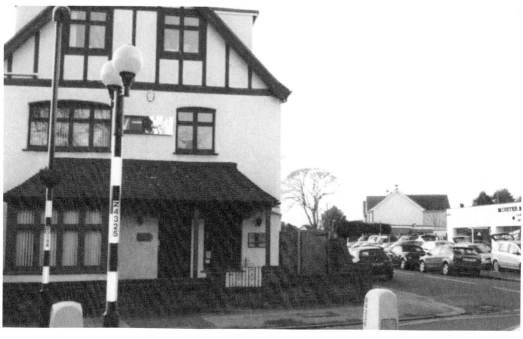

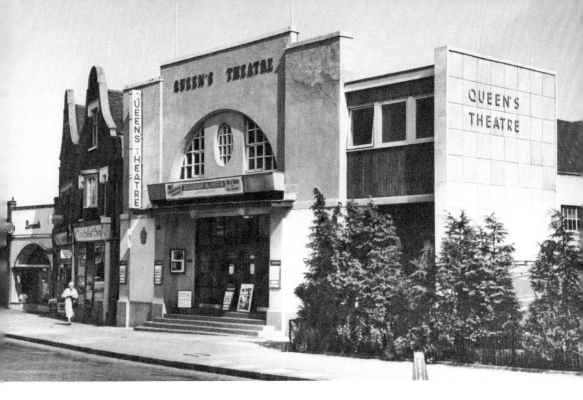

Queen's Theatre

The Queen's Theatre in its original premises the revamped Hornchurch Cinema in about 1960. Hornchurch Urban District was "one of the few local authorities in the country which has displayed such enterprise". This referred to what had been appropriately opened in Coronation Year, 1953 – a theatre described by Sir Ralph Richardson as "a beauty being created". A new theatre was built in Billet Lane in the mid 1970s.

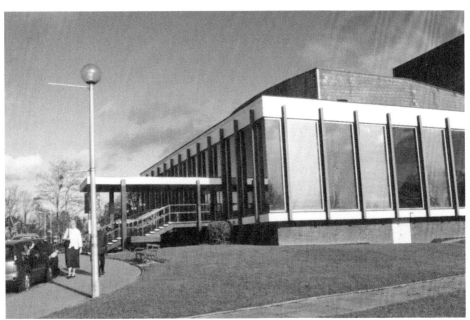

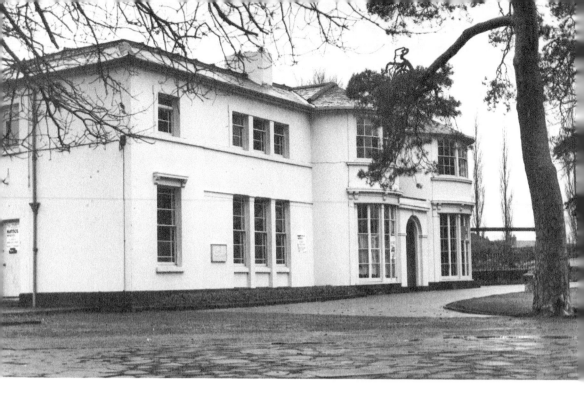

Libraries Old and New

Harrow Lodge seen in the 1960s has been Hornchurch's original public library, opening in 1936. A new library was opened in the 1960s in North Street and a recent photograph shows the completely revamped building, with modern lift and stair tower. This is the centre of a multitude of activities including a Citizens Advice Bureau, many new library events, music evenings and the meetings of the local Historical Society.

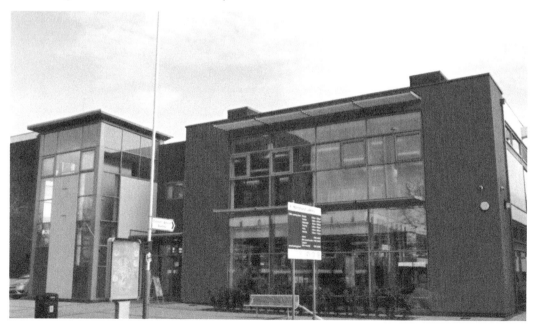

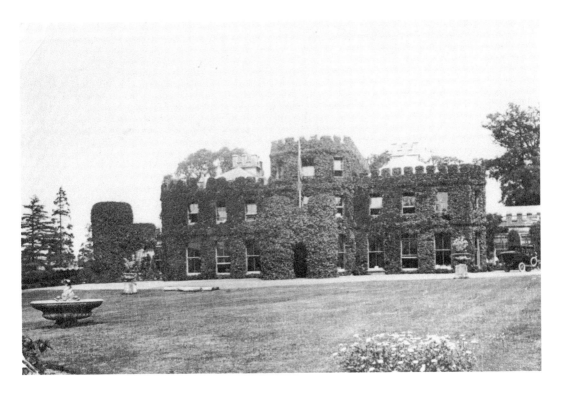

Grey Towers

An early motor car stands outside Grey Towers Mansion at right. This view originates at a time when New Zealand officers had taken over the house and grounds. On the left is an interesting dolphin-style fountain. In modern times the fountain has stood in the garden of a house in Keswick Avenue, built after Grey Towers was demolished.

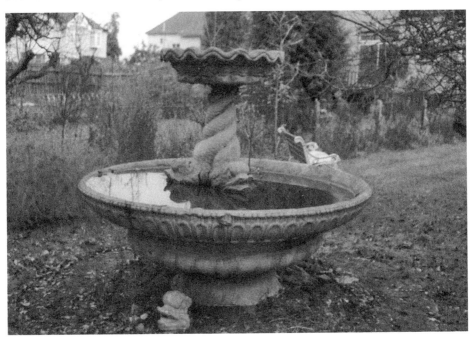

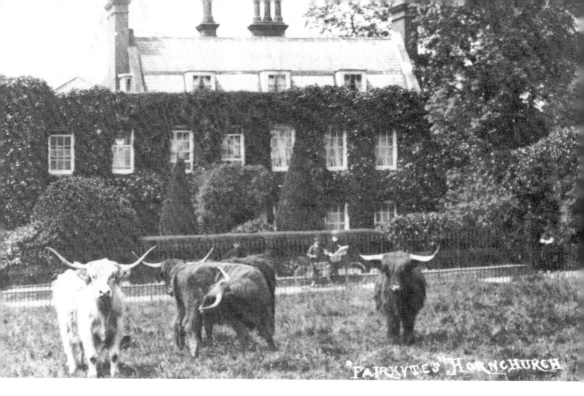

Fairkytes

While horned cattle graze in front and look up in surprise at the photographer, Fairkytes, a survivor from the eighteenth century, stands covered in foliage, obscuring some of its features. The house became an Arts Centre in the later twentieth century, which hosts a large number of societies involved in a great number of artistic endeavours. Various parts of the house have been restored in line with the original state as far as possible. Previous uses have included functions of Hornchurch Council and as a public library. The son of Elizabeth Fry lived here in the nineteenth century.

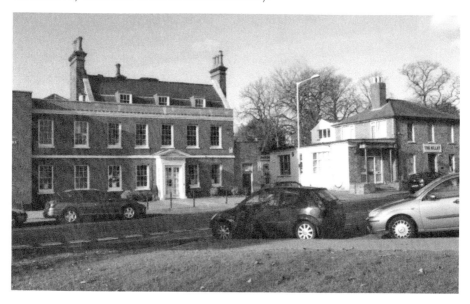

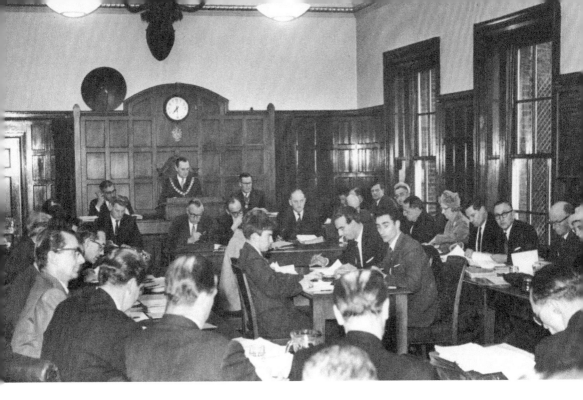

Meetings at Langtons

Hornchurch Urban District Council in session in Langtons Mansion in the 1960s. Mrs Fraser Parkes gave the mansion to the fledgling council in 1929 when the separate administration was only three years old. It had formerly been part of Romford Rural District Council. A modern picture shows the beginning of a session of the Havering Historic Environment Forum, at which local groups confer with representatives of the London Borough of Havering.

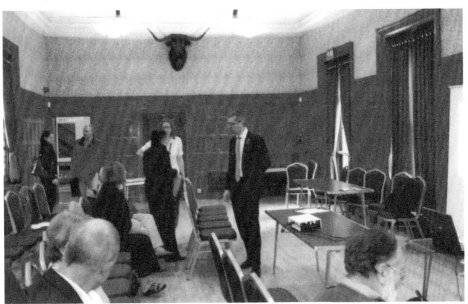

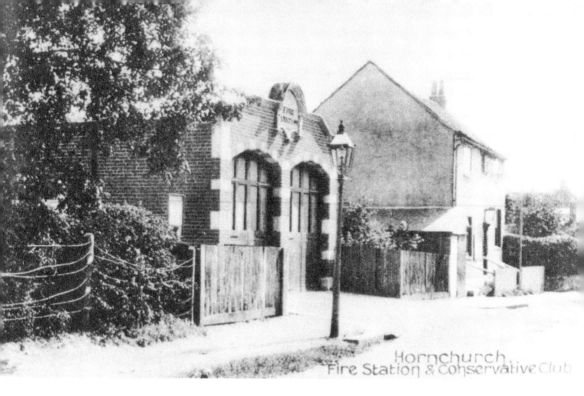

Hornchurch,
Fire Station & Conservative Club

Fire Station

The former Parish Fire Station in Billet Lane was sited next to another historic building which mysteriously burnt down several decades ago. The site is now absorbed into the Sainsbury's store and part of its Car Park. The modern fire station in Billet Lane has on several occasions been the subject of the threat of reduction or abolition.

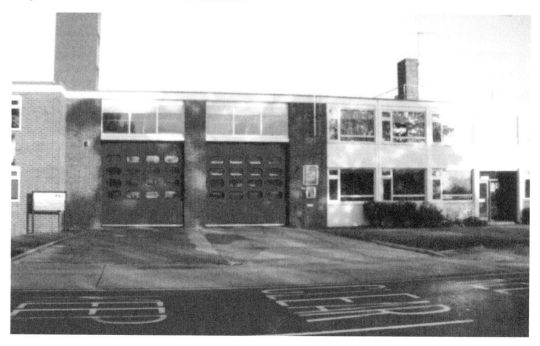

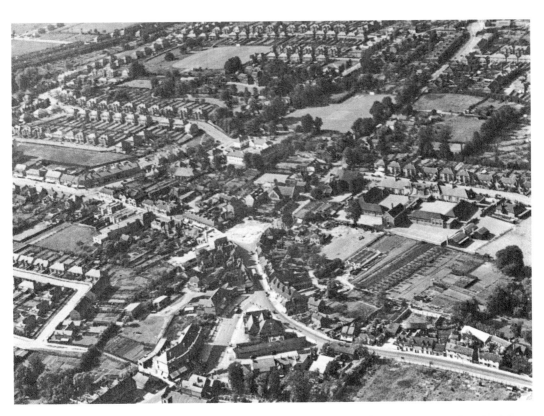

From the Air

An aerial view of Hornchurch about 1938. The old Britannia building has been demolished, and the former brewery site lies empty. Fentiman's nursery behind the High Street is neatly laid out and clearly visible. Looking out over Hornchurch as a crane hovers for the topping out ceremony of the Queen's Theatre in 1974.

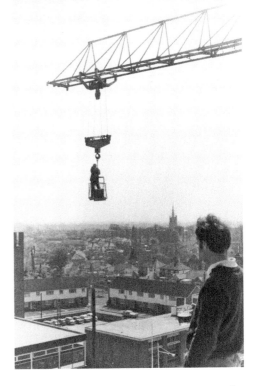

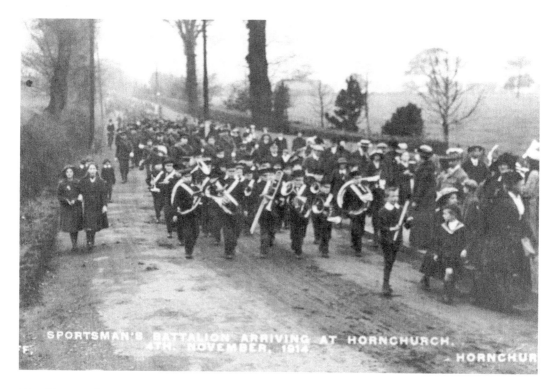

Marching Bands

The Sportsman's Battalion marching down Grey Towers Hill, led by the St Leonard's Children's Home Boys Band, on arrival at Hornchurch, 4 November 1914. The green fields of the Grey Towers Estate and its surroundings show what is being fought for at the beginning of World War I. A splendid marching band perform in a celebration on the Queen's Theatre green, continuing the tradition of youth bands begun at St Leonard's.

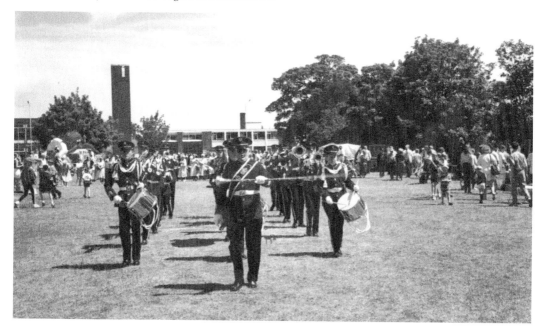

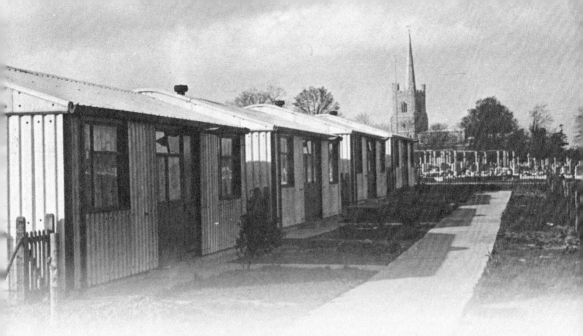

CHAPTER 5

South

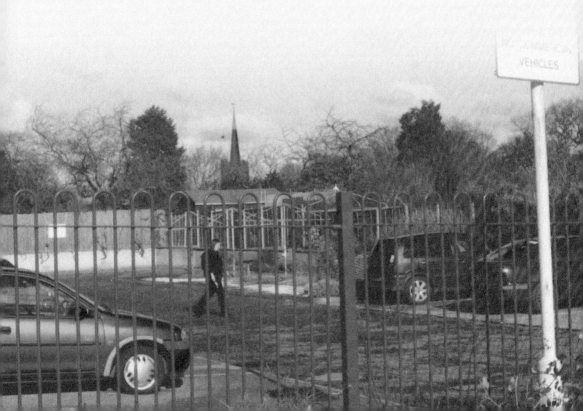

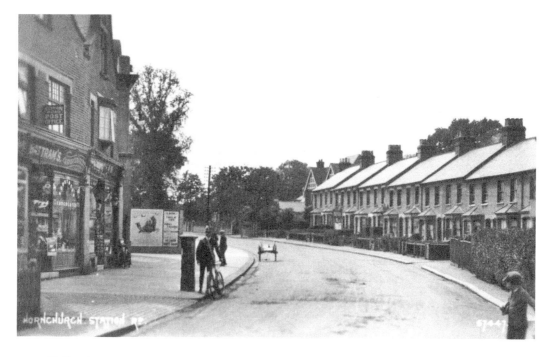

Station Lane

In the late 1920s the Hornchurch town centre end of Station Lane, then called Station Road, is seen stretching away in an arc of Victorian houses on the right. The shops on the left side include Battrams confectionary store and Post Office, complete with a post box and postman outside. No moving traffic is visible. Today the street is 'noisy' with road markings and street furniture as well as traffic. The left hand block has been rebuilt, and in between the photographs the Queen's Theatre has come and gone.

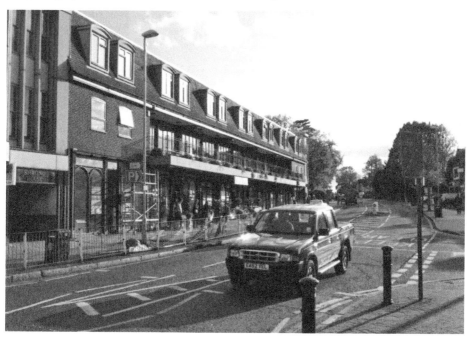

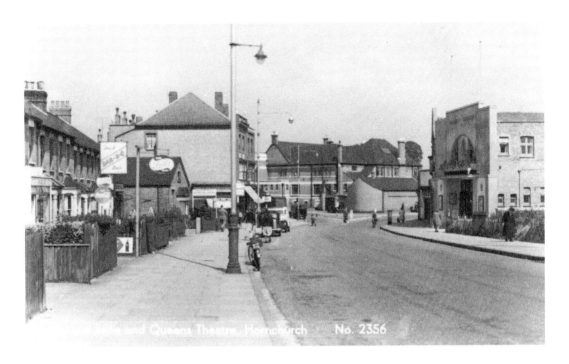

and Queens Theatre, Hornchurch   No. 2356

Station Lane, Looking Down

Looking back down Station Lane in the early 1960s we have the beginning of the commercialisation of the arc of houses pointing towards the White Hart in the centre – Pepsi and Coca Cola are being sold from a premises. Across the road on the right is the Queen's Theatre founded in 1953. The premises still bear the look of the cinema for which the building was originally constructed. Today service activities and traffic are in full swing.

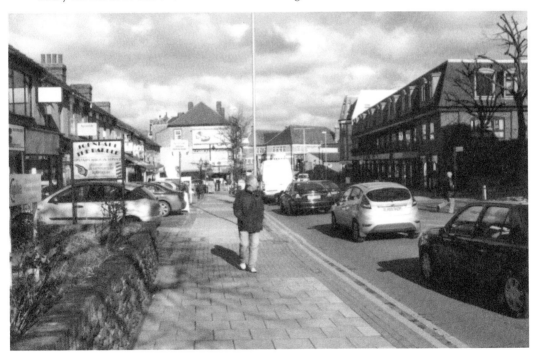

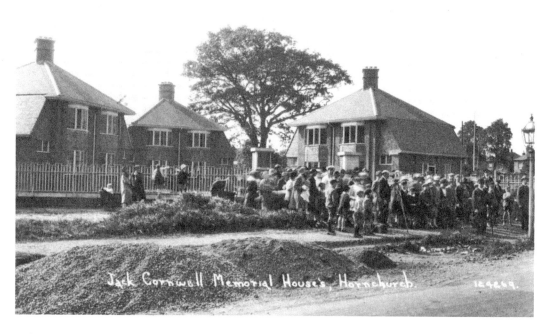

Jack Cornwell Memorial Houses, Hornchurch.

Jack Cornwell Memorial Houses

A crowd of people with a cameraman are present at the ceremony, probably the opening of the Jack Cornwell Memorial Houses on Station Lane. Today a plaque on the entrance gate records that these homes were one of the practical memorials to the boy sailor VC, and were opened by Earl Jellicoe on 31 May 1929. The homes were to be let to disabled sailors and/or their dependents. Today the houses have settled into the landscape and a sapling outside has become a tree.

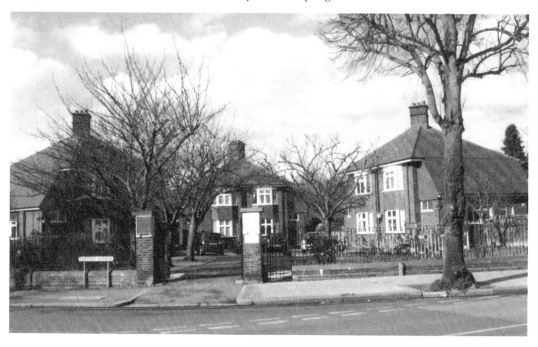

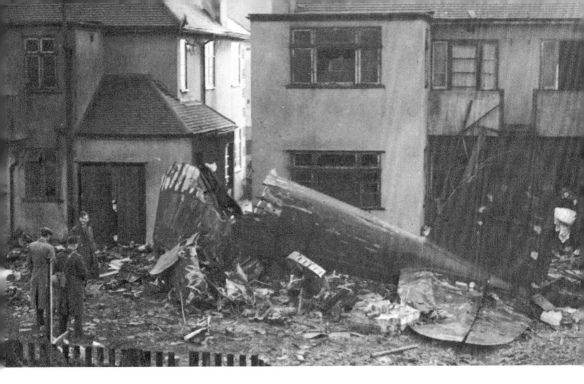

Crash!

In the parlance of RAF pilots of the time – "Raider down!". The wreckage of the Heinkel III at Matlock Gardens off Station Lane which fell to earth on 1 November 1940 after anti-aircraft fire from Chadwell Heath gun site. Unfortunately petrol spread over an air raid shelter and a husband and wife and their two year old daughter died. Two flats were demolished and several damaged. The peaceful scene today on the spot where the plane was within a few feet of plunging into the railway cutting by Hornchurch Station.

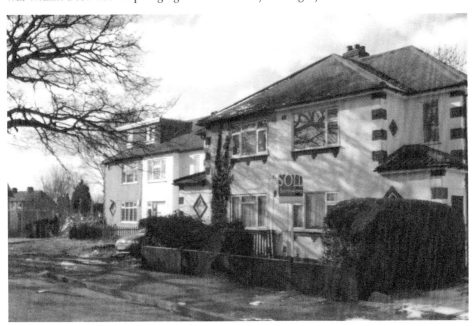

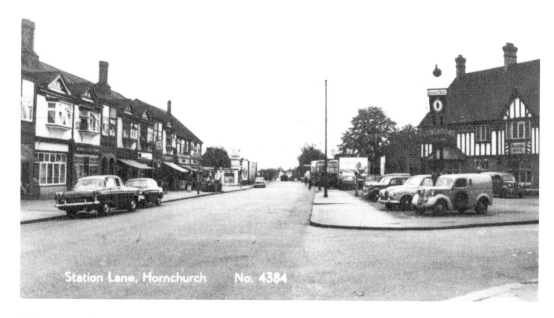

Railway Hotel

Early 1960s Station Lane by the Railway Hotel, which is offering luncheons. Two buses on route 66 stand outside the station. Motor car traffic has already grown as shown by the parked vehicles. A modern view of the hotel, which now has bollards guarding the car park and an outside garden.

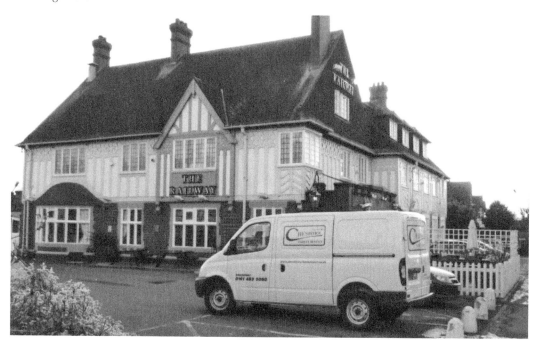

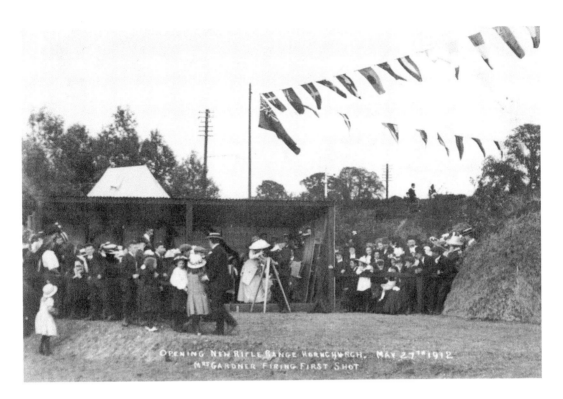

OPENING NEW RIFLE RANGE HORNCHURCH. MAY 27TH 1912
MRS GARDNER FIRING FIRST SHOT

Rifle Range

This delightful view of adults and children is of the opening ceremony for a new rifle range on 27 May 1912. Adjoining Hornchurch Station it had an ideal situation below road level in an old mineral working. Local notable Mrs Gardner is firing the first shot. Today houses occupy the frontage and their rear elevations are on the lower ground.

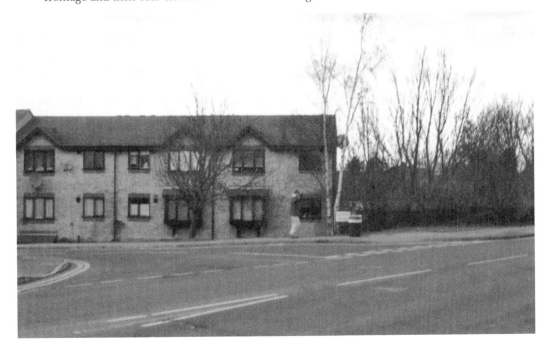

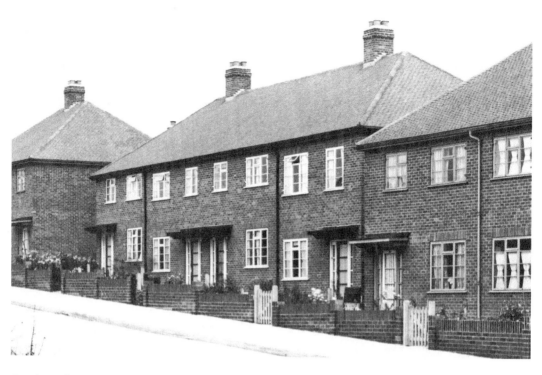

Goodwood Avenue

223 to 229 Goodwood Avenue represent postwar housing shown in its early years of occupation. Designed by Hornchurch Urban District Council's staff to a good standard, it sits on a sloping site – not a motor vehicle in sight. The scene today.

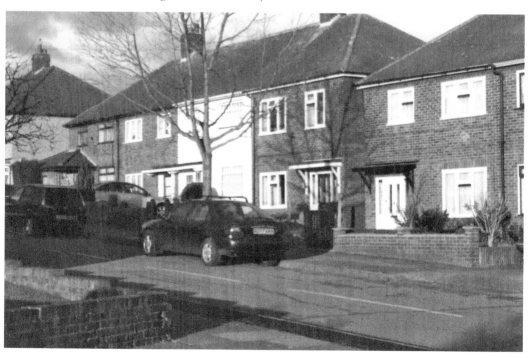

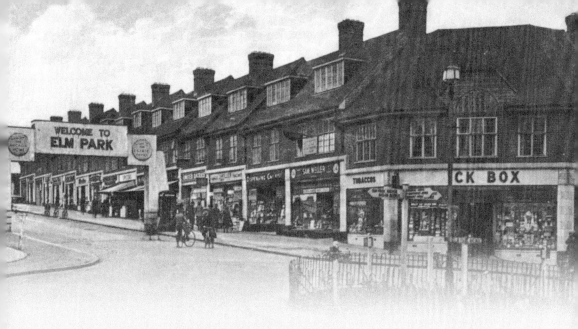

CHAPTER 6

Elm Park

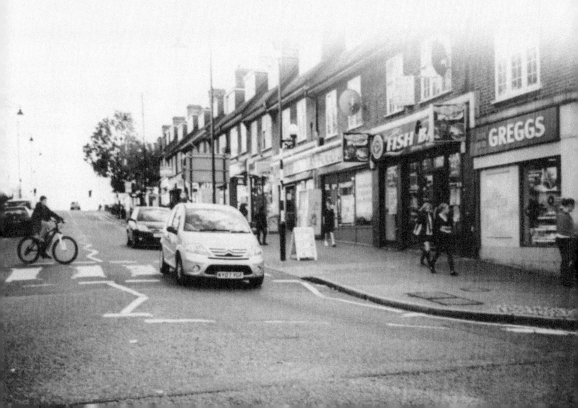

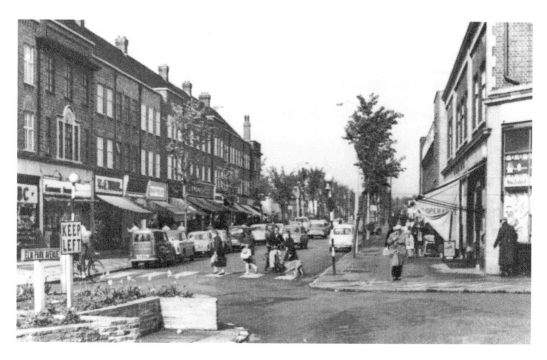

Elm Park Avenue

Elm Park Avenue (East) presents a lively scene in the early 1960s with ABC, Economic Stores, Maypole and even a Woolworths along the parade on the left. The Co-operative store trades from its corner site on the right. Today a Tesco Express has joined the shopping parade, and there are still some smaller businesses plus a modern Co-op out of sight on the right. A typically massive road sign and a delivery vehicle obscure features of the scene.

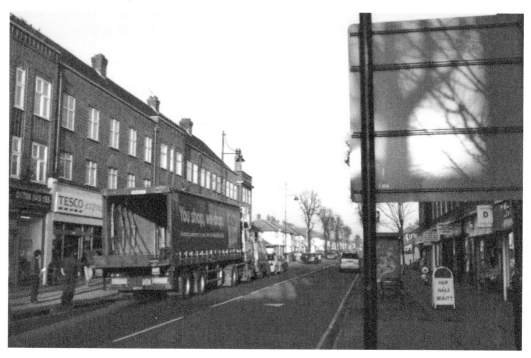

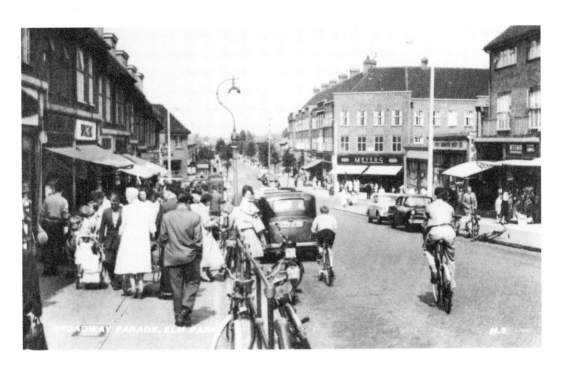

Cycling in Elm Park

Cycles are a favourite form of transport proceeding down the slope from the station in the late 1950s, but there are also many pedestrians. Individual shops in Elm Park are close to much of the original housing and still do good trade while large supermarkets are still to make an impact. In recent times local shops have to fight against the movement to one stop shopping in supermarkets slightly further away. A modern cyclist follows the cars down the slope, in between the typical modern businesses.

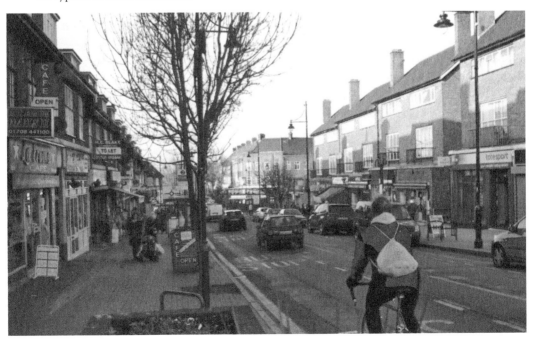

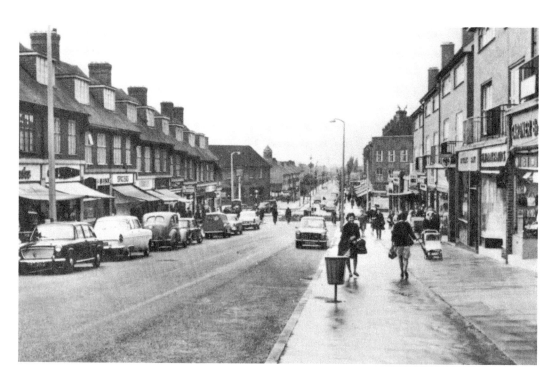

Broadway

On a wet day in the 1960s housewives are hurrying along to complete their purchases. A view from the east side of the Broadway shows Gardner's, Elm Park Florists and Barclays Bank on the right. Across the road the line includes Bata's shoe shop and Spicer's behind a row of parked vehicles facing in both directions. Today the road is crowded with cars and the 365 route bus taking locals to Hornchurch and Romford.

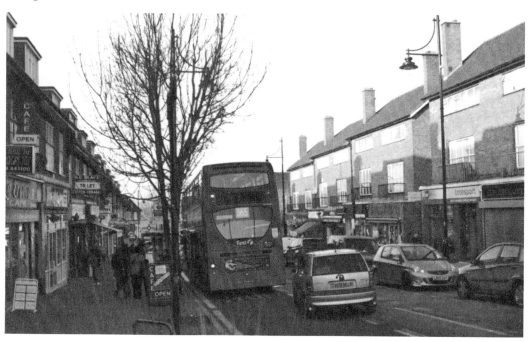

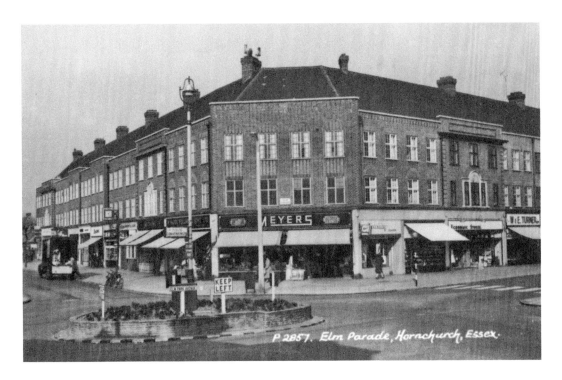

Elm Parade

In the 1950s the junction at Elm Park bore signs asking motorists to keep left – although they are not much in evidence here, some may have been unused to the roundabout system. Shopping still appears to be a sedate occupation enshrined in the phrase "just popping down to the shops". Today the roundabout has a sponsor and a notice warning that CCTV is in operation. Fast food shops have made an appearance.

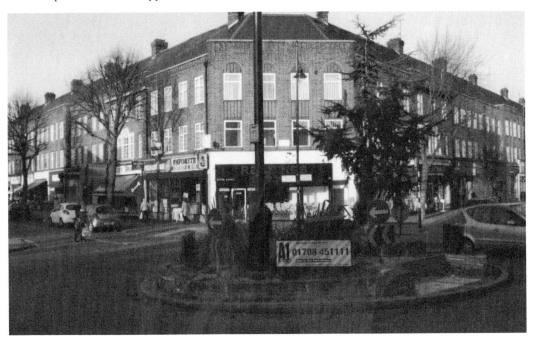

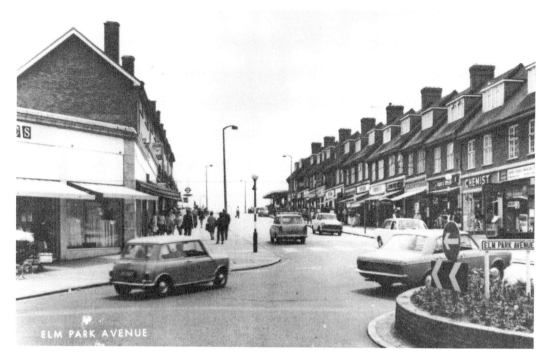

Crossroads

In the 1960s the Co-op store selling curtains and fabrics occupies the south east corner of the junction. A Mini type and other cars hurry on their way up the Broadway. A London Transport totem style sign points to the station at the top of the rise. Sidney Dean and Weaver – Estate Agents, United Dairies and Spicer's are still trading amongst a good range of goods and services still in business. Today Elm Park Pharmacies have taken over the corner site, which still has a Co-operative store presence to the left, and several bits of street furniture have appeared including a rubbish bin and a post box.

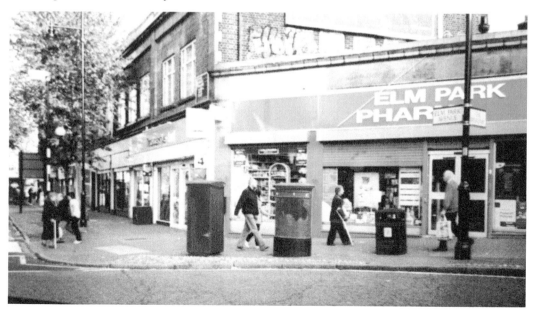

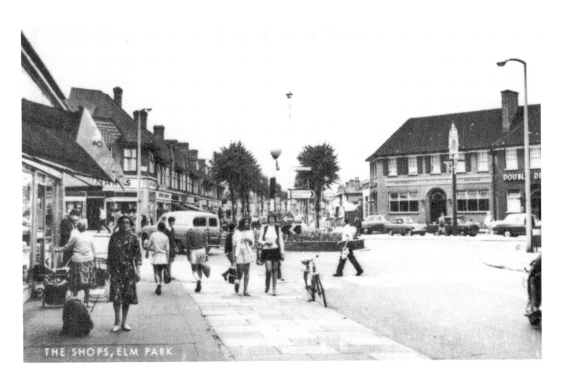

THE SHOPS, ELM PARK

Elm Park Shops

Looking towards the cross roads from the eastern part of Elm Park Avenue, Elm Park Tavern in the right distance, a lively shopping day features a lot of activity, including two young ladies wearing the mini-skirted fashion of the 1960s. The sign on the roundabout points to the library and free car park. A Vespa type motor scooter is entering the shot from the right. A clutter of lighting poles and street furniture partly obscures the late winter afternoon scene today.

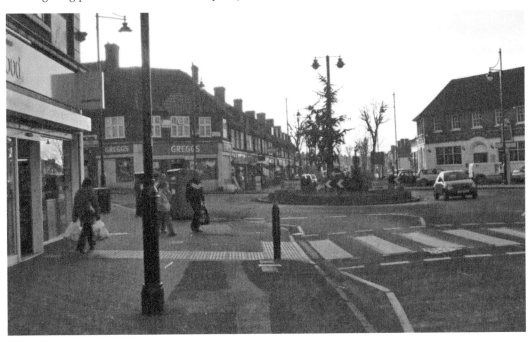

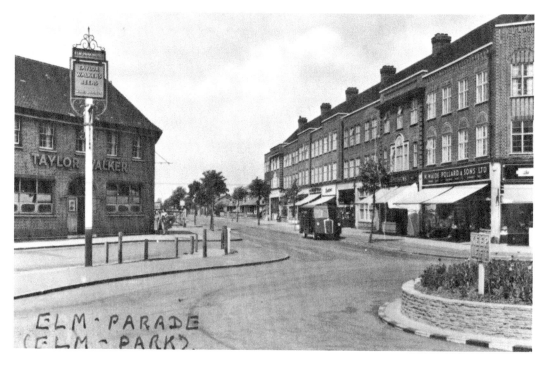

Elm Parade

A quiet day at the junction, looking down St Nicholas Avenue (originally known as Timmings Way after 1935 and before the church was built). Two ladies stroll past the Elm Park Hotel, which is a Taylor Walker concession at this stage in the 1950s. A Commer van waits outside the shops of Elm Parade, where Wade Pollard's local branch has a good site near the corner. The Keep Left sign on the roundabout now has reflectors to assist visibility. In 2010 a fast food shop has replaced Pollards and the original saplings have grown in height, reaching towards the high level lighting standard poles.

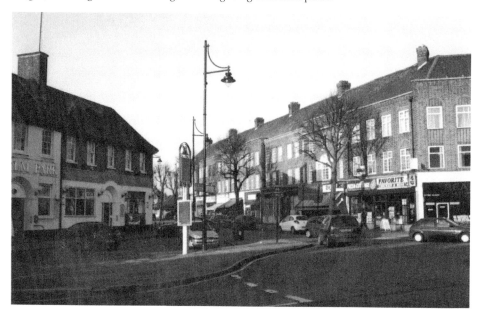

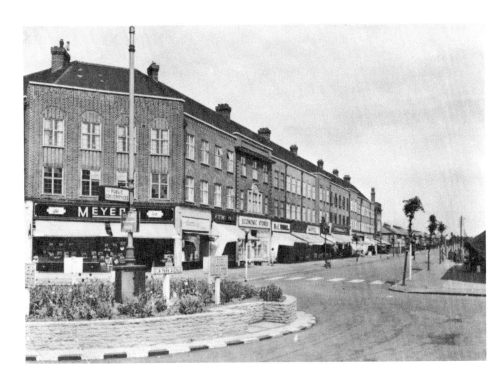

Elm Park Avenue

A view across Elm Park Avenue – from the eastern end in the 1950s to the shops and houses beyond. The careful spending habits of pre-war and post-war Britain are reflected by the presence of the Economic Stores and F. W. Woolworth, who departed Elm Park sometime before their recent national demise. Today not all of the sapling trees have survived the rigours of increasing traffic.

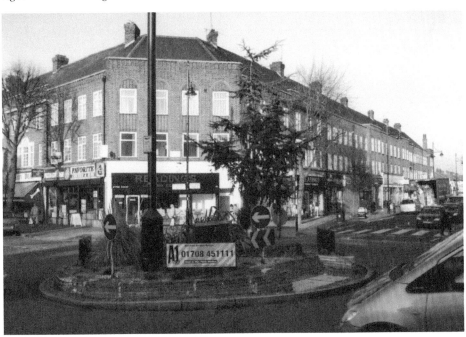

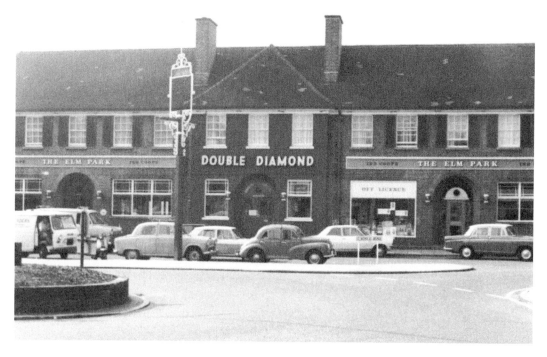

The Elm Park

In this 1967 photograph the Elm Park hostelry displays the Ind Coope logo and a prominent advert for Double Diamond. The premises also contain an off licence on the right hand side. On the left the then current version of a white van seemed less threatening. A repainted and refurbished public house offers live entertainment and home cooking.

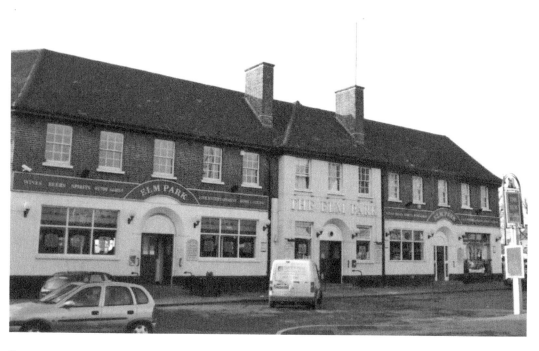

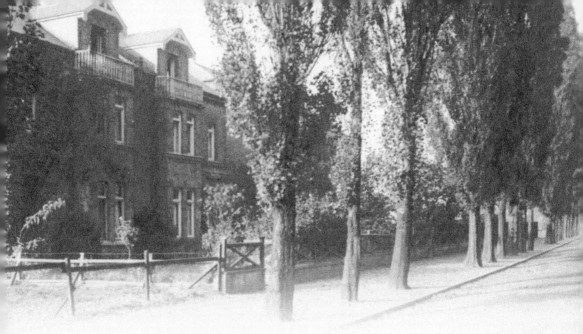

CHAPTER 7

Harold Wood

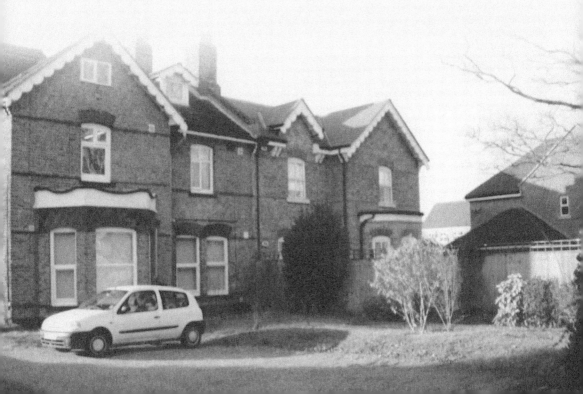

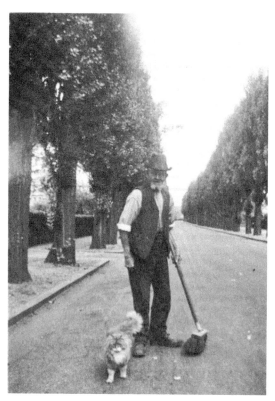

Street Cleaning
Mr Martin, the local road-sweeper, with his friend Ginger White Boots keeping an eye on the operation in the 1920s in Avenue Road. A recent view of the avenue with its trees and grass verges and newer housing at the beginning of Church Road. A street care vehicle pauses on its daily round.

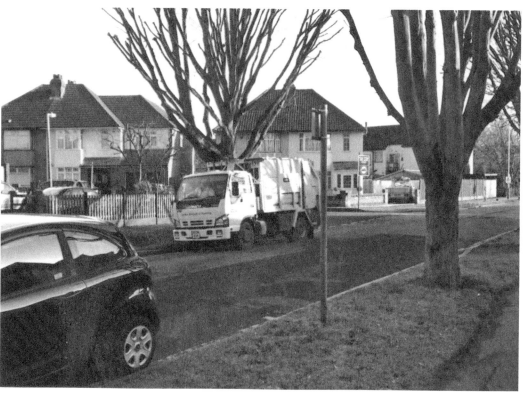

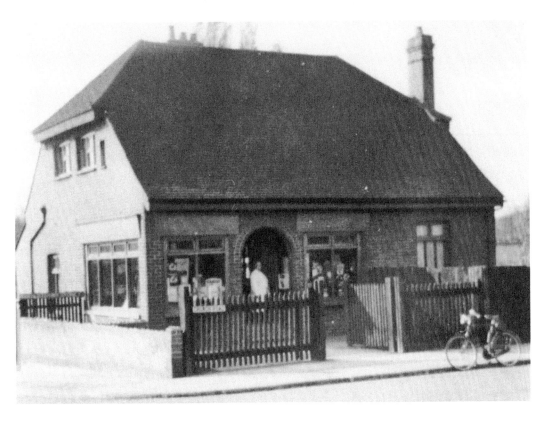

Local Shop

The local store at the corner of Church Road's eastern end, was a useful convenience in the days before local car travel was common. It was only a short walk or cycle ride from many of the neighbourhood houses. The building still exists but no longer as a shop – in the meantime further adjacent housing has been built.

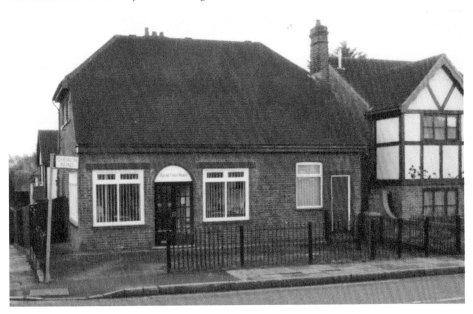

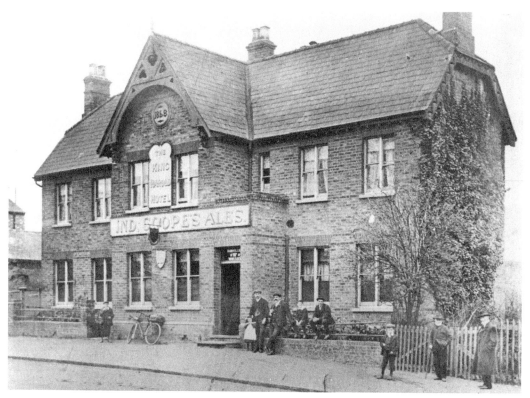

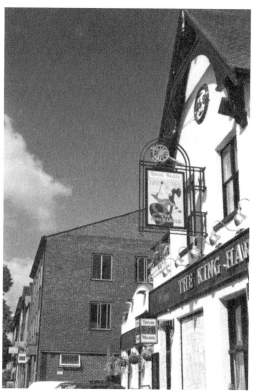

The King Harold

Four children are among the adults pictured watching the photographer prepare to record the frontage of the King Harold public house about 1910. A sign outside proclaims that this is a cyclist friendly place of refreshment. Everybody except the little girl is wearing some kind of hat. For a while in the late twentieth century the pub was decorated on one wall with a representation of King Harold based on the Bayeux Tapestry, recording the many distant historic links of the whole local area.

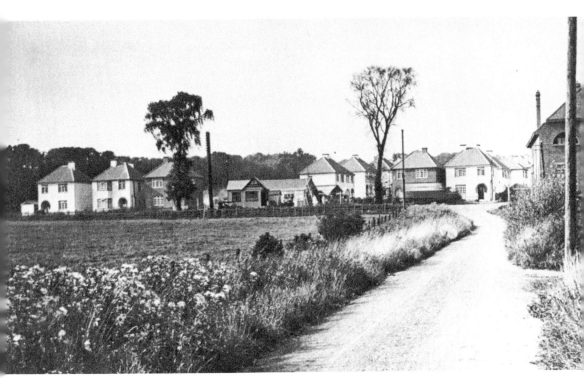

Harold Court Road

Wild flowers grow on the side of Harold Court Road looking north to the new Sunnytown houses and the Colchester Road. At the right of the picture is the Dutch and Little building, said to have been originally planned as a hotel. Today's view encompasses an interesting short parade of shops, bus stop and shelter and the Dutch and Little building now commercial premises. A premises below this has retained the title Airport Engineering, harking back to the days of Maylands Aerodrome just to the east.

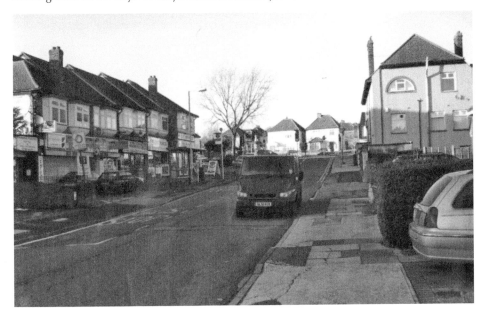

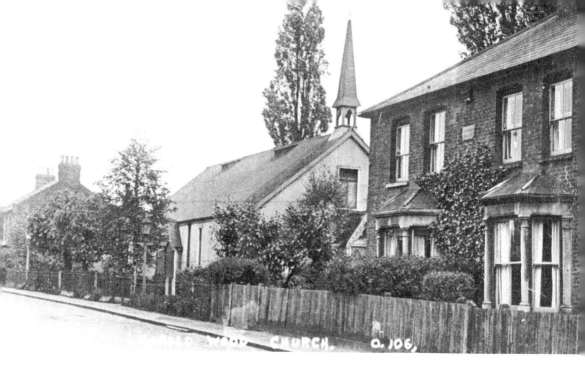

Church Road

The original tin church and some of Harold Wood's Victorian housing are seen in this photograph in the early twentieth century. The church was built in 1871. A new church on a plot in Gubbins Lane, that had been purchased in 1909 was opened just before World War II, on 4 March 1939. Although the church has moved, Church Road still bears its title, and extensions, refurbishments, new town houses and other types of housing now line this Harold Wood artery.

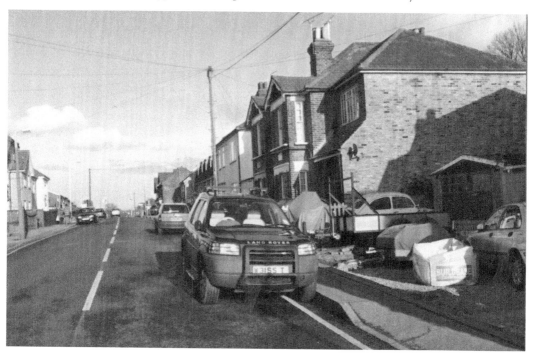

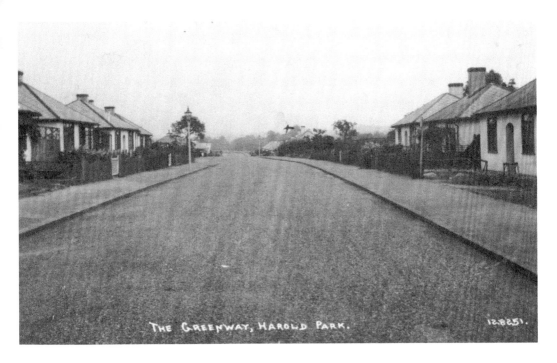

THE GREENWAY, HAROLD PARK.

12.8251.

The Greenway

In the late 1920s – the Greenway, a recent Sunnytown development sits quietly on the edge of the built up area. At the time bungalows were a very popular as well as an affordable style of home. In recent decades the area has retained its popularity, but often the homes have been extended sideways and upwards.

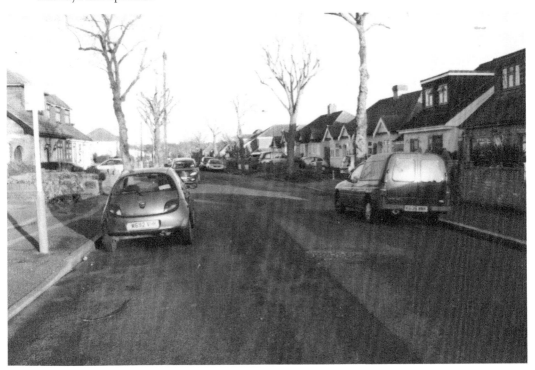

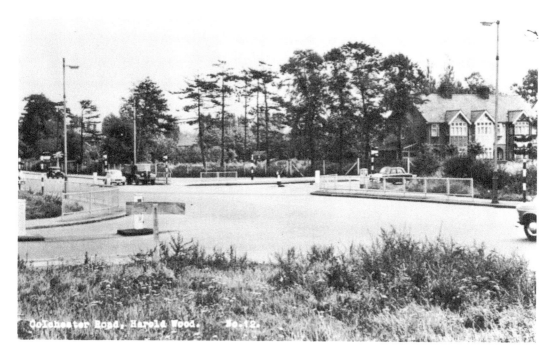

Colchester Road, Harold Wood.   No.12.

Gubbins Lane

A 1950s view from the northwest corner of the crossroads looking towards the houses at the top of Gubbins Lane. Notice the quaint but less obtrusive street furniture of the time. The rough grass in the foreground is now part of the eastbound carriageway, as the road was extensively widened a few decades later. Gooshays Drive on the left was also widened making a straighter route across to Gubbins Lane. Looking in the other direction from Gubbins Lane today the houses seen in the earlier picture are still on the right with a new block of flats beyond.

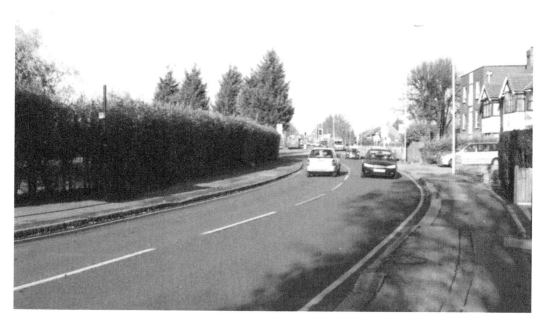

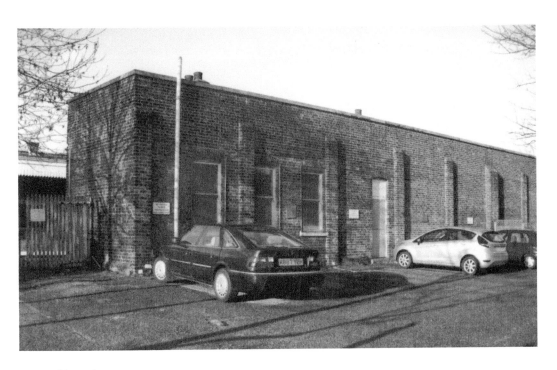

Old Station

The remains of the old station entrance at the junction of Oak Road and Fitzilian Avenue and Athelstan Road on the far side of the line. Today's new entrance, constructed on the down side accompanied the quadrupling of the tracks, completed in the 1930s. This service is busy at peak times with Harold Wood commuters travelling to employment in London.

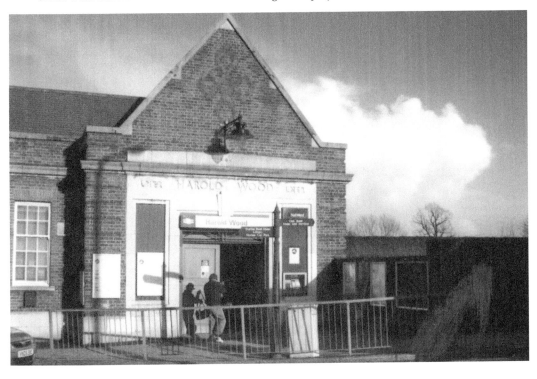

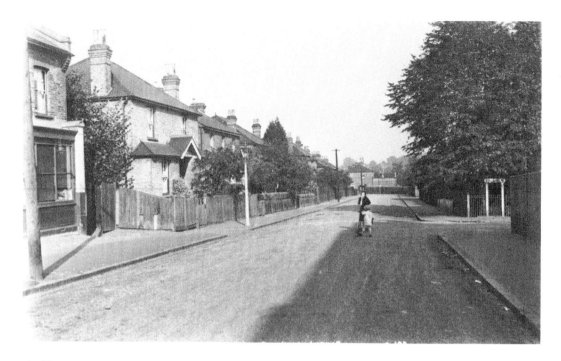

Fitzilian Avenue

Fitzilian Avenue about 1920 showing the end of the shopping parade on the left, north, railway side which faced other shops on the south side. Most of the immediate needs of the local populace were served by these outlets which included a post office. The solitary gas lamp was one of a number rather widely spaced. Family life was more based on the home than today, explaining the quietness of the scene. Now a squadron of cars are available to carry members of the family to leisure pursuits and a wide range of public activities.

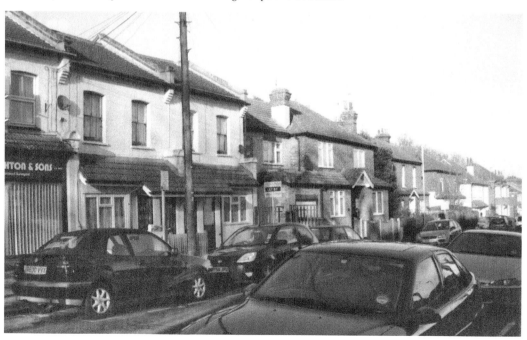

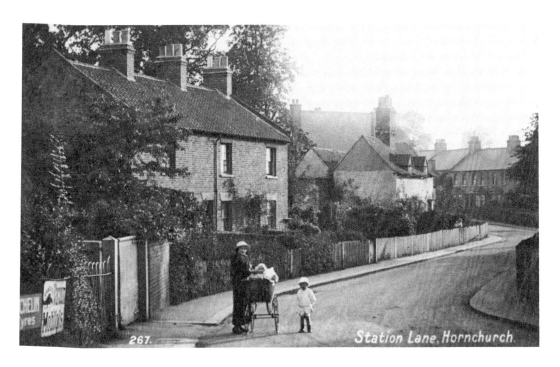

267. Station Lane, Hornchurch.

Station Lane

Goodbye to old Station Lane Hornchurch behind the White Hart in the early 1920s. A mother stands with her two children, one in old style of pram, in the roadway without fear of approaching traffic. Towards the right of the delightful curve behind the White Hart there is what appears to be a much older house than the Victorian dwellings on the left. Centuries before pilgrims bound for Canterbury may have departed Hornchurch via this route. Now high buildings from three centuries overlook the busy traffic scene.

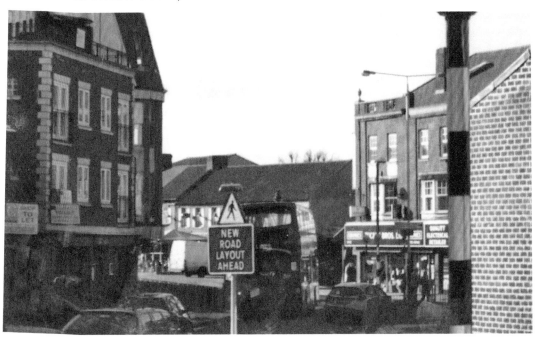

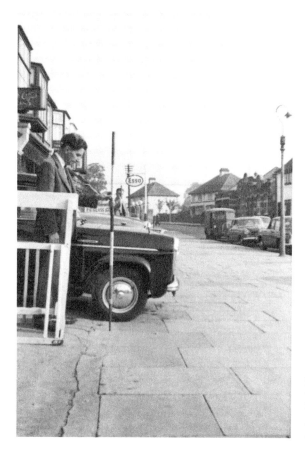

Billet Lane
At the garage at the bottom of Billet Lane two men with poles appear to be measuring the extent of their property. Across the road is the old fire station and firemen's houses.

Acknowledgements

Charles Frost, Andrew Muckley, Peter Welling, Roy Squire.
    The author apologises for any omissions.